# Regifted

# Regifted

An Adoptee's Memoir of True Belonging

Candi Byrne

SHE WRITES PRESS

Published 2022
Printed in the United States of America
Print ISBN: 978-1-64742-279-0
E-ISBN: 978-1-64742-280-6
Library of Congress Control Number: 2022907119

For information, address:
She Writes Press
1569 Solano Ave #546
Berkeley, CA 94707

She Writes Press is a division of SparkPoint Studio, LLC.

*Dedicated to the Blessed Virgin Mary,*
*and to the Duchess.*

"*True belonging is the spiritual practice of believing in and belonging to yourself so deeply that you can share your most authentic self with the world and find sacredness in both being a part of something and standing alone in the wilderness. True belonging doesn't require you to change who you are; it requires you be who you are.*"

—Brené Brown, PhD, MSW, Braving the Wilderness: The Quest for True Belonging and the Courage to Stand Alone

# Part One

*In all of us there is a hunger, marrow deep, to know our heritage—to know who we are and where we have come from. Without this enriching knowledge, there is a hollow yearning. No matter what our attainments in life, there is still a vacuum, an emptiness, and the most disquieting loneliness.*

—Alex Haley

# Chapter 1

I wound my way through farmettes with no-frills clapboard houses, big oaks and maples, and open fields—the Midwestern landscape of my childhood—none of the pinched feeling of the East Coast, where I'd lived most of my adult life.

Siri piped up: "In one mile, turn left. Then the destination is on the right."

My anxiety red-lined. "What the fuuuuuuuuck are you doing?" I gasped, then swerved into the parking lot of a fire station. My hands shook as I switched off the car; my stomach felt like a bingo-ball machine.

Yesterday morning I'd been sipping coffee in my dining room, gazing at the heavily wooded acreage sheltering my mountainside home in West Virginia. Innocent. No idea I was just hours away from making a six-hundred-mile drive to solve a lifelong mystery.

"I can't do this. I'm not ready. I'm not ready. I'm not ready," I keened, rocking back and forth in the confines of the driver's seat. Black spots pulsed in front of my eyes, keeping time with my racing heart. I stabbed at the window button, and earthy air bathed my face. Thick and fresh, infused with the smell of late spring, fecund and loamy. I pulled the oxygen-rich air into my lungs, feeling it working through my system—green juice extinguishing the hot anxiety.

My sporty Toyota hummed, sighed, and clicked. My breathing

slowed. Black spots subsided. Bingo balls ceased percolating. The sun warmed my left side. *Maybe I'll just sit here like a lizard, basking without a worry.*

*Or you could just turn around and go home.*

Deep breath. Then another. "You could . . . but you're not, Little Missy." I clicked on the radio and scanned the stations until I heard NPResque content. Familiar. I needed to ground in the familiar.

After a few minutes of news, I reached for the innocuous manila folder that had been riding shotgun—my "black ops" file. The folder held six pages, printouts about several women I'd gleaned through BeenVerified, a paid database of names and contact information. Information that had been denied to me implicitly for fifty-two years and explicitly for a half dozen more.

Information that thanks to an unexpected—and freaky—call hours before from my ninety-two-year-old Aunt Dolores, brought me one mile and a left turn from ambushing my birth mother. My birth mother whose name had been legally kept from me all my life. My birth mother who, for the past six years, had vehemently denied contact with me.

The firehouse bay door rattled and shimmied open, revealing an imposing fire truck with a chrome-bumper underbite—my cue to beat feet before well-meaning first responders came over to check on me. Back on the move, my heart accelerated as I headed toward the unknown. *I'm gonna do it. I'm gonna do it. Gonna get the answers.*

The houses were closer together and nearer the road as I approached the town. American cars. American flags. American Midwest. Sturdy, basic, uncomplicated. Families. Generations. I knew this place—I was *from* this place and space, but not *of* it.

I'd always yearned to know that I carried the DNA of strong, cre-ative, eccentric, wise women. A legacy I could cling to and genetics I could count on to buoy me up and through times of doubt. My adoptive maternal grandmother was a bootlegger, slumlord, and entrepreneur. My adoptive mother followed in her mother's footsteps, but in larger, more extreme ways. Stories of their lives and accomplishments were exciting and inspiring . . . but I was not of their blood. They were step-stories, no more related to me than stories of Eleanor Roosevelt or Wonder Woman.

I wanted a family homestead—the place where all the relatives had gathered for celebrations over the decades. I ached for extended family with cousins as friends and the bedrock certainty that an Aunt Thadwina would tease an Aunt Kitty about her lopsided icebox cake, and that an Uncle Baxter would sport seasonally appropriate novelty ties.

I wanted to have people. To be of a people. To be one of the bright stars in a constellation of people, twinkling in and among the other stars. I longed to have strong roots, deep roots, grounded roots to sustain and support me as I grew and thrived. I wanted to be a honey crisp apple among all the other honey crisps.

But I was a watermelon grafted onto an apple tree. I was a fruit—beautiful, juicy, and full, appealing in my own way—but I was not and never would be a honey crisp. Same with my adopted brother and sister. We were a Frankenfamily, the seams evident and ill-fitted together. It always felt like we were the obvious evidence our parents' branches could not bear their "own" fruit. Were we not included in extended family functions because of my parents' embarrassment over their fruitlessness, or because of the judgement or discomfort of other relatives? While going through paperwork after my adoptive father died, my siblings and I found evidence that his parents had left money to all their grandchildren except for the three of us bastards.

Individually, family is so important to me, my sister, and my brother—we each have circled the wagons around our respective spouses and offspring to create of-ness, but we don't intermingle. In the past forty years, our three families have gotten together exactly once.

I slowed for the blinking light at the main intersection in Buchanan, Michigan. I'd gone through this intersection dozens of times during my formative years. From what I'd gleaned in the past two days, my birth mother had lived and worked all her adult life just a couple dozen miles from where I'd grown up in South Bend, Indiana. Had I ever passed her on the road? Flicked through blouses together on the same rack at Kmart? Sipped on milkshakes in adjoining booths at Bonnie Doon's?

Would I know her if I saw her? I once saw a woman at a national conference who so looked like me—zaftig, cropped auburn hair, spatulate fingernails—I was convinced we had to be related. I was terrified to approach her; did I or did I not want to know we were blood kin? What would I say? "Uh, yes, excuse me, but did you or anyone in your family lose something? See—big keister and bright blue eyes—remind you of anyone?"

I cruised down the street, where according to BeenVerified, my birth mother, Mary, lived. The report revealed Maureen, Mary's oldest sister, also lived on this street a few blocks away. As I scouted the neighborhood, I knew there would be problems maintaining a low profile. This was precisely the kind of small town where everyone participated wholeheartedly in the neighborhood watch committee. In other words, a community of busybodies who would most definitely notice a big redhead driving a candy apple–red foreign-made car with out-of-state tags . . . especially if that big redhead resembled their friend and neighbor, Mary.

I drove at a sedate pace through the enclave of modest ramblers

with detached garages and backyards big enough for vegetable gar-
dens and games of horseshoes. Mary's house was Monopoly-sized,
painted off-the-shelf white from Sears, with a concrete front stoop.
A faux gas lamp burned even in the daytime. Did that mean she was
gone for the day, or just unconcerned about her utility bill?

Her scrap of front yard appeared freshly scalped. *She's in her late
seventies; did she do that herself? Her sister Maureen's husband? A
late-in-life love?* The driveway, two parallel cement tracks set into the
lawn, was empty. The garage door was closed, its five small panes of
glass covered in black paint, cloaking whatever was inside. I knew
the thick springs on the door would protest upon opening, even if I
were brave enough to risk checking inside for a car in broad daylight.

I continued down the street to scope out Maureen's house. The
homes at her end of the street were larger—two-story brick with lush
lawns and complex landscaping. Most every yard had a blue Dickies–
wearing homeowner wielding yard-improvement implements or
vehicle-sprucing equipment. *It is noon on a workday. Why are all
these people home?!*

I cut shifty eyes as I neared Maureen's address. A lean man paced
the lawn behind seed-broadcasting cart. *That's gotta be . . . well . . .
my uncle.* I had a sudden urge to pull into his weed-free driveway and
announce myself: "Yoo-hoo! I'm hooooome."

I drove on.

At the next cross street, I turned right, then right again, driving so slowly the speedometer didn't register. I craned my neck and
bobbed and weaved my head to see if I could get a peek of Mary's
backyard. My movements were so herky-jerky, I feared the neighbors
would call for the paramedics, certain I was having seizures.

These secret-agent moves felt ridiculous. I was preparing to
dive-bomb into Mary's life—a life that, as I'd learned through the

adoption agency—had never included even a mention of me to her family. It was unlikely then that she would have shared the news with the neighbors. No matter how I felt about her choice to remain silent, it was her choice, and I felt an obligation to respect it, even if it meant going to these absurd lengths to honor her privacy.

I idled for several minutes at the corner, contemplating my next move. I marveled at an elderly gent carving his front yard into impeccable stripes, deftly pivoting his red Wheel Horse lawn tractor into perfect alignment with the previous pass. One, two, three times. *How much longer are you going to sit here?* He turned for a fourth slice and frowned under the brim of his high, square gimme cap. *Uh-oh.* I flashed him a thumbs-up and a grin. His face softened; then he lifted his chin in acknowledgment and motored on.

I flipped down the visor mirror and eyeballed myself. "Well, Byrne, she's either there or she's not," I said to my reflection.

"Brilliant observation," I retorted, then slapped up the visor. "All right, girlfriend," I encouraged myself, "lez do this thing. No guts, no glory."

A moment later I was parked on the pea-gravel shoulder in front of Mary's house, wishing I'd packed a paper bag to breathe into. I got out of the car and steadied myself. My legs shook, bent, and bowed, as unstable as pipe cleaners holding up a bowling ball. My hands trembled, making my clutched keys sound like a tambourine.

*Keep going. Keep going. You're okay. You're okay. You're okay. Almost there. One knock and it'll all be over,* my mind looped as I walked up the sidewalk to the stoop.

*Come on, one step, another step. One. Step. Another. Step.* Standing at the front door, hyperventilating, I noticed a rustic-looking wooden welcome sign, the kind you'd buy at a Cracker Barrel or from a retired guy who made dozens of them in his garage while his wife crocheted dolls with voluminous skirts meant to hide a roll of toilet paper.

Welcome. Would I be welcome? Maybe. I was prepared for anything that happened once I knocked. Tears. Hugs. Recognition. Confusion. Anger. Fear. Weapons. Couldn't control any of it. Only thing in my control was knocking on the door.

For years I'd said I wanted to connect with my birth mother if only to say she wouldn't have to worry I'd show up on her doorstep someday. And now here I was. A bolus of anger rocketed through me. *Well, she's had pah-lenty of chances to prevent this. It's her fucking fault I'm standing here now. If she had just sent me one fucking photo! If she had agreed to talk to me just one fucking time, I would not be standing here!*

I snorted short fast breaths. Like a bull. *Like the Taurus you are.* A breeze blew. Birds serenaded. Mr. Wheel Horse took another lap. Finally, calm claimed me.

I raised a now-steady hand and knocked.

# Chapter 2

G rowing up, I sorta liked the idea of being adopted. Aside from my brother and sister, I knew no other adoptees; it made me feel unique, almost exotic in the company of the kids from blue-collar Polish, Serbian, and Hungarian families that populated South Bend, Indiana. My past was a mystery, while theirs was . . . well, pedestrian, predictable, and a little hard to pronounce with the dearth of vowels in their Eastern European surnames.

I had a passing curiosity about my birth parents but no urgency to seek them out even in the worst teenage years when I railed against my adoptive parents ("You're not my *real* parents") and ran away at age sixteen, sharing a house with a pot-smoking, third-rate guitar player whose four cats peed in the butter dish.

The impending birth of my first grandchild, Corrina, due in March 2009, shifted my perspective; I was seized by the need to learn if there were potential genetic time bombs lurking in my DNA. I'd been cavalier about the lack of medical history when my kids were born—I was young; ignorance was bliss. Older and arguably wiser, I couldn't bear the idea of my children and grandchildren being blind-sided by a diagnosis that could have been predicted or prevented.

My two siblings and I were born in the United States in the mid-twentieth century—the era of sealed adoptions, which makes gleaning identifying information about birth families as difficult as buttoning a blouse while wearing boxing gloves. In the majority of states, privacy—secrecy—in favor of the birth family prevents an adoption agency from revealing personal details unless the birth parents explicitly and proactively give permission or the birth parents are dead.

In the summer of 2008, my brother, Peter, brought up the idea of initiating the search for his birth mother. He'd seen the movie *August Rush* and sobbed when he spoke of the title character, who'd been given away and whose mother was told August had died at birth. August spent his formative years in an orphanage, his wide eyes and guileless expression emphasizing his belief that his parents were looking for him. My brother knew with every certainty that his birth mother had not willingly given him up—he *really* needed to believe that.

Michigan is one of forty states where adoptees are denied access to their original birth certificates. With no way of knowing the names of the birth parents listed on that important piece of paper, Peter turned to Catholic Charities, the agency that had handled each of our adoptions. He learned that even in the digital age, the adoption files are still in analog form—paper-based and on microfiche—so he needed to identify the specific Catholic Charities office that had handled his adoption. According to our amended birth certificates, we'd been born at Wayne County General Hospital in Detroit, Michigan. Catholic Charities offices ring the Detroit metropolitan area, so it was difficult to pin down the correct office.

Once he'd found the right location, he received in short order a letter rich with non-identifying information about his birth family, including the shocker that he was of mostly Irish descent, not the German lineage he'd been raised believing and his blond hair and Teutonic personality supported. The social worker who'd prepared the letter, Loretta Colton, was known as a Confidential Intermediary (CI)—a person sanctioned by the state to access sealed adoption files, glean and share non-identifying information, and broker contact between willing adoptees and birth parents. The CI serves as middleman until both sides are willing and comfortable to make contact directly.

It was a no-brainer—he wanted Catholic Charities to track down his birth mother and initiate direct contact. Along with their social work responsibilities, CIs are detectives—while they can see identifying information in the adoption files, the information is not updated after the adoption is final. Birth mothers will likely have been married, changed addresses, or, in some cases, died in the ensuing decades.

Loretta found Peter's mother, Barbara, right away. And Barbara really *had* been looking for him for years. He learned she had indeed been coerced into relinquishing him. I never spoke about it with Barbara, but I imagine she'd been force-fed the party line—"forget him and get on with your life; you'll have other babies." In a twist of fate, she wasn't able to have other biological children though, and ended up building her family through adoption.

Shortly after Peter received his non-identifying information, my sister, Maggie, and I submitted our respective non-identifying-information requests, along with the $120 fee. My letter from Loretta arrived in my West Virginia home several weeks later, on the same day my sister's letter arrived in her South Florida home. We'd agreed to open them at the same time. Maggie started reading from her letter: "birth mother gave birth to a son six years before I was born. Birth mother never married . . . late thirties, had kept the boy. Oh! There's a history of Crohn's!"—Maggie's oldest son had been hospitalized for that very condition. "Huh . . . says the birth father was never told about her pregnancy with me."

My letter from Loretta was disappointingly skimpy—scarcely two pages with only the barest of details. My birth mother was the second of nine Irish Catholic children. Her father was a draftsman, her mother active in civic organizations and the church. My birth mother suffered "unspecified trauma to the head" during her own birth and "her muscular and motor development were slow."

One sentence jumped out at me: "She did not know the father."

I felt frustrated and disappointed. Pissed. Though Peter's and Maggie's respective birth mothers hadn't told the birth fathers about their pregnancies, each mother did know the identity of the baby daddy.

"She did not know the father? What does that mean?" I asked Maggie rhetorically. "Maybe that the football team gangbanged my developmentally challenged birth mother and there was no telling which sperm made the winning touchdown?" Nothing spackles over my difficult feelings better than sarcasm.

Then I mentally paused my snark—I'd been raped at the age of thirteen by two strangers; the adult me observed the momentarily regressed me judging a mentally challenged teen who may have been raped. I felt like a cartoon character with an angel on one shoulder suggesting compassion for my birth mother and a pitchfork-wielding devil on the other condemning her for being an indiscriminate slut.

The letter went on to say there was no question about the family giving me up. I took the snark off pause: "What, keeping a tenth kid would have killed you?" The pastor of the church my birth grandmother frequented apparently had a heavy hand in the decision. My birth mother did time at an unnamed home for unwed mothers, where, the letter noted, she sewed and kept to herself.

Also, I learned I was blinded in the orphanage.

During the time I crib-surfed for the six weeks between my birth and the day I was placed with my adoptive parents, I was treated for an eye infection. At age five, I underwent eye surgery to correct a lazy eye. I later learned the eye surgery couldn't have cured my vision deficiency, and, for all intents and purposes, I am blind in one eye. Little One-Eyed Orphan Candi.

I scanned the few paltry paragraphs from Loretta again, looking for clues to my endomorphic body type, my taller-than-average height, and . . . well, looking for clues to *me*. What part of me was formed by the pathetic creature sketched in the letter? And who, damn it, contributed to the other half?

Maggie and I were both eager to know more. She was ready to take the next step and request contact. For years she'd wondered from whom she'd inherited her uniquely shaped eyebrows. She wanted to meet her tribe. I had no desire to meet mine; I only wanted to know my ethnicity and family medical information, and to see pictures. We both wanted to know our respective origin stories.

The following week, my ire dampened, I wrote a heartfelt letter for Loretta to share with my birth mother if and when she found her still alive: "Thank you for life. It all worked out for the best. I'm a happy mother of two and a grandmother-to-be. Breathe easy; I'm not going to show up on your doorstep. Please share ancestry, medical history, and pictures."

# Chapter 3

In January 2010, Loretta called as I was driving home to West Virginia from Florida, newly parentless after the sudden death of my father in Orlando. "I just spoke with your birth mother," she said without preamble.

Hands shaking, I pulled to the side of the road. "She's still alive?" I said in wonderment.

"Yes, and so is your maternal grandmother," she said.

I was doing the mental arithmetic—five generations!—when she continued, "but I'm sorry to tell you that your birth mother doesn't want to have contact with you."

Traffic on I-95 zoomed by, rocking the car as I sat and processed the news.

"Did she say why?" I finally asked. "And . . . did you tell her I didn't want contact, just information and pictures?"

"She was very reluctant to talk to me at first. I didn't think I was going to get anything out of her, but I started reading parts of your letter to her, and she opened up a bit."

I heard papers rattling on her end. "Let's see . . . she's been widowed for twenty years. Was happily married. One son . . . he's the oldest. Twin daughters. Retired food-service worker. Close to her family." Loretta continued, "She said no one in her family knows about you and she doesn't want to open a can of worms."

"A can of . . . worms," I said flatly.

"She did say that she thought of you often. She was so glad to learn that you were happy and that life was good for you."

"Did you ask her for a picture?"

"Yes. She's . . . unwilling to provide one," Loretta said, her tone gentle and empathetic. "She has some disfigurement from mouth cancer, and, well . . . she's unwilling."

A convoy of semis roared past, pinging the car with road debris. My dad's car. My dead dad's Ford Focus station wagon, still reeking of the cheap cigarettes he bought from Indian casinos. I watched the numbers on the digital clock morph from seven to eight to nine before responding, "So that's it?"

"She did agree that I could call her in six months and see if she changed her mind, so that's something."

"Uh-huh."

"She named you, you know—Theresa Lynn."

"What's her name?"

"I'm sorry, Candi, but I'm not allowed to tell you."

*So now she knows all about me, and my kids, and my grand-daughter, but I know nothing more about her than I'd learned through reading the non-identifying information. I have no idea where she lives, what she looks like, or even if she really is "slow."*

"Your letter said she experienced head trauma during her birth; did she sound . . . disabled? Or, you know, um . . . challenged?" I asked.

"Did it say that?" I heard papers being shuffled. "Hmm . . . no, her speech was slightly impaired, but I imagine that's from the mouth cancer. No, she sounded of . . . normal intelligence."

I nibbled at a cuticle. "Anything else? Anything at all?"

"It was a short call. Like I said, at first I wasn't sure I'd get anything, but the call ended on a positive note. I'll check back with her in six months, but I wouldn't be surprised if I hear from her before then."

Six months later, after talking with my birth mother again, Loretta maintained optimism that she'd "come around"; six months after that, she said the same thing. My frustration grew—Loretta was in contact with my birth mother, yet I was denied my history, her name . . . even a single picture. "Can't she send one taken before the disfigurement?" I pleaded.

∾

My second granddaughter, Jillian, was born in February 2011, and from the beginning she was the very essence of my son, Kelly . . . so much so that we lovingly refer to her as "Little Daddy." Seeing the generational carbon copy brought to mind "visual echoes." We could see so much of Kelly reflected in his daughter. And there are visual echoes of me reflected in my son. But without a photographic reference to my birth people, those echoes stopped with me.

My son and daughter didn't care that there was no connection to my biological family, photographic or otherwise, but I had a visceral need to "see" my lineage. Maybe if my birth mother saw pictures of my kids and grandkids, she would be moved to share photos. I called Loretta at Catholic Charities.

"I'm sending some snapshots for you to share with my birth mother," I said. "Happy to reimburse you for the cost of postage to get them to her."

"Hold off sending them until I get permission from her," Loretta said.

"Permission?!"

"Yes, she has to agree to receiving them before I can send them."

"Why is it that she has the control in all of this? Why don't I have a say?"

"I'm sorry, Candi. I'll get back to you as soon as I talk with her."

~

My phone buzzed as I was hurrying through the community college courtyard, late for a graphic design class. I fished through my bulging pink messenger bag, then glanced at the phone screen. Loretta. I scowled at the smokers lounging against the NO SMOKING WITHIN TWENTY-FIVE FEET OF THE BUILDING sign, ducked around the corner to catch a deep breath of noncarcinogenic air, then answered.

"Candi, I'm so sorry, but I have bad news," Loretta said. *My birth mother's dead. She's got a restraining order. My adoptive mother was really my birth mother.* "I was concerned when I hadn't heard back from your birth mother in a month. Her voice mail was full, so I couldn't even leave a message."

I swallowed against the sudden lump in my throat. "Is she . . . dead?"

"No, but your . . . uh . . . her . . . son is dead," Loretta said.

I looked down at the pebbled cement and traced an arc with the toe of my Keen sandal. *"Your brother" is what she was going to say. They're dying on me before I even have a chance to learn about them.* I flared with anger. *All this bullshit delay and avoidance, and now . . . one down, how many to go?*

"How did it happen? How old was he?" I asked.

Loretta sketched the details she'd gleaned from my birth mother—she'd gone out with one of her daughters; her son stayed home because he wasn't feeling well. At some point, he cut the lawn, then came into the house, lay on the couch, and had a fatal heart attack. My birth mother found him when she'd returned home. I tried to imagine how I would feel coming home to find my son dead. Tears plopped from my cheeks to the dusty pebbled cement, creating specs in the grime.

"After his funeral," Loretta said, "she stayed with family in Florida. She said she couldn't bear the thought of living in the house where he died, so she is packing up and moving this week."

I bumped my shoulder against the brick of the building, partly to ground myself but mostly as a distraction against the bubbling inner turmoil.

"She said to tell you she's sorry, but she can't focus right now on you."

I straightened and stiffened. "All I wanted was a picture. And for her to see pictures of my kids and grandkids—*her* grandkids and great-grandkids. How much focus does that require?!"

Loretta ignored my rhetorical rage. "She did give me her new phone number. I'll try again in six months."

Dark spots blinked on and off in my vision. I imagined my blood pressure rocketing up to a level that would ding the big bell on a carnival strength test. "Six months," I huffed.

"She said she and her son were very close. She's devastated."

I paced, pivoting my feet to grind and scatter a constellation of cigarette butts. I snorted and snarled under my breath, "Damn smokers . . . too lazy and careless and thoughtless to bother to spare those of us who don't share their affinity for poisonous litter."

Loretta waited patiently and silently as I processed. After a series of deep breaths, I asked again, "How old was he?"

Muted computer-keyboard clacking. "The obituary says he was fifty-two." I did the math. My birth mother had found another man and had gotten pregnant in, what . . . two years after giving me up? And decided to keep my . . . him? What did he have that I didn't?

"Was he married? Kids?"

Her fingers tap-danced on the keyboard again. "Let's see. No, never married. No kids. He was an environmental engineer at a hospital for most of his life."

Hmm . . . an engineer? A brainiac bachelor?

"There are some lovely tributes to him in the obituary comments," Loretta continued. "Lots of them mention your birth mother."

I forced a light tone: "Oh, I'd love to read them. Would you send me the link, please?"

Loretta sighed. "Oh, Candi . . . I can't. There's identifying information listed."

*WTF?!* My anger flared so hot, the smokers could have lit their cigarettes on my forehead.

"Don't give up hope, though," she continued. "She did give me her new phone number. I'm sure she'll come around once she's over the shock of his death."

Through clenched teeth I asked that if under the circumstances, would she at least share my birth mother's first name. "It's ridiculous and clumsy for me to refer to her as 'my birth mother' all the time."

I sensed her hesitation, then said, "I'm guessing given her Irish Catholic background and birth order, she's an Anne, Mary, or Margaret."

Long silence. Then, "You could call her Anne," Loretta said.

I didn't trust myself to say anything more than a terse thank-you before ending the call. My stomach roiled. Denied and denied and denied again. A ticker of hateful sentiment scrolled through my mind: *You gave me away. You kept him. Now he's dead. Maybe God is punishing you. You kept me a secret. Secrets are toxic. Toxins kill. He's dead. No kids. You have nothing left of him. I'm still alive. I have kids.*

*Grandkids. But don't even think of turning to me, your . . . runner-up kid.*

~

I brooded through the first half of my graphic design class. Not even the thrill of creativity could quell the drumbeat of anger, hurt, and frustration. I ditched class at the break and muttered and sputtered and banged on the steering wheel as I drove home.

I *had* to see that obit. I just absolutely had to know who this guy was, needed to see his picture. Loretta had said he looked like a nice man. What does that even mean? Suit and tie? Scout-leader uniform? I brake for unicorns tie-dye T-shirt?

*Wait a minute. I'm a librarian and research girl. I can find it without her.* I used to track down fugitive literature for Congress and the White House—before the Internet, thank you very much. Finding needles in haystacks a specialty.

I booted up my Mac as soon as I got home, then made a cheat sheet with the few non-identifying details I'd gleaned from Loretta and the adoption agency:

<u>Him</u>
fifty-two years old
environmental engineer at a hospital
died at home between mid-April and late May 2011
father died twenty years ago
two younger sisters—twins
never married
no kids

Birth mother—Anne
second eldest of nine children
mother still alive
Irish Catholic
retired cafeteria lady
widowed, never remarried
high school dropout


Not much to go on. I guessed that unless Anne had married well
or married someone with more education and therefore more opportunities to leave the Detroit area, she'd stayed close to her family
roots. I added "Michigan; possibly Indiana, Ohio, and Illinois" to the
cheat sheet.

In middle school, I was smitten with a boy with the last name of
Flynn. In the time-honored tradition of young love, I punched him
on the arm and gave him grief at every turn, including referring to
him as "Flynn Phlegm." Many years later, my mother told me she
cringed every time I'd said it because "Flynn was your last name."

My mother had a Silly Putty relationship with the truth—there
was generally a faint impression of the facts, but it was almost always
distorted, twisted, or manipulated in her favor. I had no reason to
believe my mother was lying about Flynn as my birth name, but I had
no reason to believe she was telling the truth. She had, though, been
truthful about the last name of Peter's birth mother, and about the
fact that Maggie was born to an older Hungarian woman.

I added "Flynn?" to the cheat sheet. I had no idea of Anne's married name except that it was "unusual" according to Loretta. If my
mother had been telling the truth, "Flynn" would show up as Anne's
maiden name in her son's obituary.

Hours later, eyes dry and scratchy from lack of blinking, I'd read dozens of obituaries, scanning first for age, then for the number of surviving relatives. Anne was one of nine children, so I was betting there'd be a long list of kin cited in my birth brother's obituary.

No luck.

I was back at it the next day, and the next, speed-reading past the pain, sorrow, grief, mourning, and loss of hundreds . . . thousands . . . of survivors, trying to lock in on Anne Flynn "Unusual Last Name."

One week. Two weeks. Hours and hours of wading through formal, sterile prose. Syntheses of entire lifetimes rendered in one or two stilted paragraphs—Been there. Done that. Dead.

I found one possibility—a fifty-three-year-old electrician who'd worked for a hospital near Lansing, Michigan. I checked the local electrician's union website looking for announcements of brethren who'd blown their final fuse. Nothing enlightening there. I stalked the electrician's niece on Facebook, scrutinizing her "Friends" list for clues.

I studied the electrician's black-and-white obituary photo— cropped hair, strong chin, glasses. *Do I know you? Did we share a mommy?* There were Flynns listed in his obituary, but not nearly the number of relatives I needed for confirmation. And his mother's maiden name wasn't listed as Flynn.

After a month relentlessly searching all US obituaries, I called a librarian friend with access to powerful databases. "Marlie, wouldja, couldja help me, please?" She took pity and ran the skimpy details I'd gleaned. A day later she called with the disheartening news that she too could find nothing.

Another friend had long championed the idea of searching for my birth family and had the name of an investigator who specialized in adoption cases. My heart needed answers, but my bank account wouldn't support the expense of hiring an investigator. Besides, it was infuriatingly unfair for me to have to pay when Loretta had the information from the Catholic Charities file right in front of her.

Loretta told me she had my entire file on microfiche that she kept in her home office. I gnawed at that bone incessantly—*she* could see my file, but I was forbidden to see it. As a Confidential Intermediary, Loretta could stroll at will through the records—the closed records, the sealed records—of hundreds of Michigan adoptees. Loretta, a person with absolutely no relationship to me, my parents, or my birth family, could not only read every word written about us but was authorized to make decisions about what information I could have access to, as interpreted by her!

Fantasies of launching a Delta Force–type mission to retrieve my personal records played on my big-screen mental TV. A quick reverse phone check revealed Loretta's home address. I Google Mapped it . . . wouldn't take but ten hours to reach her house in Michigan. I'm sure I wouldn't be the first frustrated adoptee to show up on her doorstep. Does Catholic Charities have a SWAT team for such occasions? I envisioned stocky priests strapping on bulletproof clerical collars, carrying .357 rosaries, and breaching doors with a battering ram in the shape of a giant cross.

I shook my head to dislodge the image of the God Squad. Loretta would give me information if she could. She'd mentioned she'd been adopted and that it had taken her fourteen years to locate her birth family because of the closed adoption system. Fourteen years!

Swiveling in my chair, pivoting rhythmically on my toe, I pondered Catholic Charities' role in helping maintain secrecy around adoptions. Not all adoptions happened through the church, though adoption records in the majority of states are sealed. What was the reason for that kind of secrecy? In these states, adoptees are legally prevented from accessing their original birth certificates or learning identifying information about their birth families without explicit consent from either parent until after the death of the birth parents—which is ludicrous because how could you know they were dead unless you knew who they were?

It's not a federal law, which meant each state had to draft, pass, and defend legislation denying adoptees access. The church is powerful, but is it powerful enough in the majority of states to maintain that level of lobbying effort? I thought about how Catholic churches were closing their doors because they couldn't raise enough money to keep the roofs from leaking or to keep the lights on. Attendance was down. So were collections. If the church had the money to lobby, wouldn't they use it to gain access to federal funding or subsidies for Catholic schools . . . or at least to patch the damn roofs?

So, who else had deep-enough pockets and the power to affect legislation in all those states? Who was so motivated to keep records sealed, to deny the civil rights of adoptees? And why? Within an hour, I had the answer. And it made me so angry I heard my soaring blood pressure thundering in my ears.

The National Council for Adoption—a pro-life movement in disguise. Their convoluted logic—if the women seeking to relinquish children for adoption knew that the children could someday learn of their biological parents, those pregnant women would run out and get abortions rather than face the guilt, shame, recrimination, and regret over their "mistakes."

Guilt, shame, recrimination, and regret may have been the prevailing climate and reality in the three decades known as the Baby Scoop Era. But in this day and age? The only ones perpetuating the myth of girls gone bad who wreak havoc on the pristine reputation of their parents are the judgy conservative hypocrites who preach "family values"—shorthand for "the Big Ol' Sky Daddy will smite you for not adhering to arcane edicts handed down from paternalistic fist to paternalistic bible-thumping fist." The fire-and-brimstone, eternal-damnation, don't, don't, don't exclusionary God must have the best public relations firm around—otherwise, who in their right mind would throw their lot in with such a heavy-handed and punitive dictator?

What do pro-lifers feel we adoptees are going to do to our birth families? Totter up on arthritic baby boomer knees and hurl invective for giving life? Demand an inheritance? Insist on photoshopping us into family photos?

~

Two months into my obit obsession, I gave up searching for my birth brother's death details. I'd drawn on every bit of librarian skill I had; if I hadn't found it by now, I wasn't going to find it. And . . . I was done. Done chasing my birth mother, done begging for answers, done with the whole damn thing. I chose to be done. I was at peace with being done.

"Maybe she'll come around," friends would say.

"Maybe she will, but she'll be there alone because I. Am. Done."

Several months later, I listened to a voice mail from Loretta; she was retiring and handing my case off to someone else. Great—another complete stranger who had full and open access to the information I couldn't touch. When the new social worker called to introduce herself and talk about my case, I told her that if she spoke to my birth mother to please tell her that no one from Catholic Charities would ever contact her again.

"So, you're saying you want me to close the case?" she asked.

"Absolutely." I felt so free in officially pulling the plug. I was in charge. I was calling the shots.

For two years.

Then my Aunt Dolores had a vision.

# Chapter 4

I was putting away laundry when my cell phone rang. It was the standard ring, not any of the personalized ringtones I'd created for those on speed dial. "Who dat at nine o'clock on a Saturday night?" I checked the caller ID and raised an eyebrow. Aunt Dolores. Uh-oh. Dolores was the ninety-year-old sister of my mother, Delphine, and she very rarely called and never at night.

"Hi, Aunt Dolores. Is everything okay?"

"Candice? Is it too late to talk?" she asked in her quavery, Parkinson's disease–affected breathiness.

"Not at all. I'm surprised to hear from you so late though."

"I had a vision," she said. Aunt Dolores, a devout Catholic, had had visions all her life—she saw and talked to all manner of apparitions. "I saw Delphine's adult head on your body—your body when you were a child. You were a beautiful child, you know, like a model."

"Best of the lot, right?" I joked.

"Yes." No smile in her tiny tinny voice, just certainty.

I sat on the bed and hitched up a knee. "Hmm. Mom's head and my body. What do you think your vision means?"

"I think it means you should look for your birth mother again."

Uhboy. Aunt Dolores remained disappointed on my behalf that my birth mother had repeatedly refused to provide information. "Oh,

25

Aunt Dolores, you know what I've gone through trying to get answers all these years. I'm out of options."

A moment of silence. "You should *never* give up. *Never* give up looking for her!"

I was surprised—shocked, actually—by her vehemence. Between the Parkinson's and her age, my aunt barely spoke above a whisper, but she'd delivered her pronouncement in a voice stronger and clearer than I'd ever heard come from her.

I mentally sighed. "Aunt Delo—"

"*Promise* me you'll never give up!"

God . . . that voice . . . was she channeling Delphine? I stood up and groomed the bedspread, smoothing out the butt wrinkles. "Okay. I'll give it another shot." *Or not*, I thought.

My insincerity must have leaked through. "*Promise*," she boomed.

Flustered and flummoxed by her Great and Terrible Oz tone, I stammered out a promise and hung up.

The following morning, I looked out through the kitchen window as I waited for the coffee to brew. The trees in the holler were fully leafed out, creating the sense that I was in a green womb. A jam session between robins and cardinals sounded through the screen doors.

Creamy coffee concoction in hand, I parked my butt on the exercise ball I'd started using instead of a chair at my desk and, heaving a heavy sigh, flipped open the laptop. Sipping as I waited for the computer to boot up, I pondered telling Aunt Dolores, "I tried, but still no luck. . . ." But I couldn't lie to a sweet old lady who'd stayed up well past her bedtime to tell me about her vision. I just couldn't.

I flexed my fingers theatrically then googled "Michigan obituaries." A familiar list of sites stacked up on the screen—the ones I'd spent so many hours scouring after my birth brother had died. "Not gonna find anything; just keepin' a promise," I muttered. I selected mlive.com and entered "Flynn" into the name field. I'd last searched in 2011 to no avail, so I entered 2012 as the earliest date to search.

Or at least I'd intended to. My right ring finger stuttered and my pinky reflexively hit return before I could correct "2010" to "2012." *Oh well*, I thought, *it's not like I haven't read a million obits already. What's the harm of reviewing a couple dozen Flynns I'd previously made my acquaintance with?*

The first search result featured a photo of a Black man I'd remembered from the last obituary-reading marathon. The second result was for Elizabeth A. Flynn, age ninety-two. I screwed up my face trying to recollect if she was one I'd auditioned before. I'd been looking for fifty-something males, not female nonagenarians. With a shrug, just like hundreds of other times, I counted the children listed in the obituary.

Huh. Nine.

Second child: "Mary (the late Martin) Matusak." Loretta had said my birth mother had an unusual name. *Matusak* qualified. "Husband dead." Loretta had also said I could call my birth mother Anne. *But . . . this is not Anne.*

I remembered from the non-identifying information I'd received from Catholic Charities that my birth mother had more sisters than brothers. I counted Elizabeth's daughters: seven. Two sons.

*Elizabeth was my . . . birth grandmother?*

*So Mary, not Anne, is my birth mother's name? Mary is my birth mother?*

*Yeah . . . has to be.*

My hands started shaking. I'd found her.

My stomach throbbed and burned. I'd found her.

I couldn't stop the tears and sobs. I'd found her. I'd fucking found her. Booyah! I'd. Found. Her. No hiding from me now!

I snagged a tissue and blotted my eyes then blew my nose.

*Gotta be sure.*

I entered "Matusak" and "2011" into the search box.

I read: "John Allen Matusak, age fifty-two, son of (the late) Martin Matusak and Mary (Flynn) Matusak. Died at home on May 6, 2011."

Ding.

Ding.

Ding.

Gulped some coffee. Reached for the phone. Speed-dialed my daughter, Caity. "Can you meet for breaky?"

Over sunshine skillets at Bob Evans, I recounted the details of Aunt Delores's vision and the results of the obituary search. "It's miraculous is what it is," I said.

Caity tick-tocked her head, one side of her mouth hitched at an if-you-say-so angle. "Whaddya gonna do now?" she asked. "Call her? Write her?"

I paused from buttering a biscuit and waggled the knife. "I'm gonna do the one thing I said I'd never do: show up on her doorstep and not leave until I get the information I want!"

Caity raised a perfectly plucked eyebrow and then nodded. "You go, girl. Any idea when you'll make the trip?"

"Tomorrow."

～

I called my son, Kelly, on the way home from breakfast with Caity to recount Aunt Dolores's vision and my plans to confront my birth mother.

"I thought she didn't want to have contact with you," he said.

"She doesn't. But . . . she's had plenty of opportunities to give me the answers I want without having to be in contact." I waved a thank-you to the eighteen-wheeler who'd high-beamed permission to merge onto the interstate. "I've played by her rules for six years . . . hell, fifty-eight years," I continued. "It's my birthright to know basic biological and genetic information."

"So, you're going to ruin an old lady's life so that you can have closure?" His tone was harsh . . . judgmental.

I squinted and frowned. "Ruin? It's not like I'm going to pound on the door and yell at her. I'm going to be gentle about it."

"Well, what *are* you going to say?" he pressed.

I flicked on the turn signal and eased onto the off-ramp. I blew out an exasperated breath, "I don't know yet. This just happened this morning. I'll have six hundred miles to figure it out."

I could picture him shaking his head, disapproval puckering his face. "I don't think this is a good idea. But I guess you gotta do what you gotta do."

Next up: my sister. "I'm going to Michigan tomorrow to meet my birth mother," I said when she answered the phone. "I need you to go with me."

# Chapter 5

Five years earlier, in late 2009, my sister, Maggie, had received a second round of information from Catholic Charities, this time with the identifying information about her birth family. Maggie's birth mother, Helen, had died from complications of Alzheimer's six months prior to the Catholic Charities' search for her. Maggie declared she wanted to track down the half brother she'd learned about to get details about the circumstances surrounding her birth.

"He's not going to know the story," I told her. "It's better to reach out to a female relative or friend who was around and aware during Helen's pregnancy."

Because Helen was dead, Catholic Charities could share her full name—Helen Irene Nagy. It took me just a few minutes on Google to find contact information for Helen's two sisters . . . and for Maggie's six-years-older half brother, David.

"Are you going to call one of her sisters?" I asked Maggie.

"I don't know! What if they don't know about me? What if they are mad that I'm trying to contact them? What if they don't want to talk to me? And 'Nagy' . . . what nationality is that?" she asked.

"I don't know for sure . . . but Mom always said you were Hungarian."

"What if . . . what if they are gypsies . . . or . . . carnies?" she squeaked.

I laughed till I choked. "If that's the case, I guess they wouldn't have a problem coming to visit you in the off-season."

∼

Helen's sister was warm and welcoming when Maggie made the initial call, and she arranged for her to talk to David. Maggie called to debrief me after her conversation with him. "He was a little miffed I didn't call him directly," she said. "I tried explaining why, but he didn't seem to get it."

"That's a strange reaction," I said.

"I thought so too! Oh well. He's sending me pictures, so I'm excited about that."

A flash of envy shot through me. *She's getting pictures.*

"Oh, and there's two."

Confusion. "Two . . . pictures?"

"No . . . two brothers."

I scrunched my nose. "I don't understand."

"Helen had three children over the years, but she only kept one, the oldest one—David. She gave up the second one, Mike, when he was born two years later, and then gave me up when I was born two years after Mike."

"Wow! Why wasn't the second one—Mike?—mentioned in the letter from Catholic Charities?"

"I don't know. But get this: David said we all have the same father . . . a married guy, who has three other children with his wife . . . and David said there may be more kids from other women."

"Wow . . . that birth father of yours is a real sharpshooter!"

∼

Over the next few months, Maggie talked frequently with her newly found brothers. All three of them wanted to meet in person; David and Mike lobbied for her to travel from South Florida to their homes near Detroit. "I'll go with you," I told her. "Fly into Baltimore; I'll pick you up and we'll head west." I wondered how I might have felt had Maggie found sisters instead. Would I have been so willing to participate in the reunion?

After hugs at the Baltimore airport arrival area, Maggie and her thirteen-year-old son, Ryan, stowed their luggage in the back of my silver Ford Focus, and we hit the road. Maryland melted away. Pennsylvania's curvaceous landscape gentled into flat Ohio vistas. As we veered north from Toledo into our birth state, our conversations were peppered with manic giddiness and what-ifs: "What if they hate me?" "What if I hate them?" "What if they won't answer my questions?" "What if they really aren't my full-blooded brothers?" "What if that guy isn't my birth father?"

We arranged a code word to invoke if any of the three of us felt uncomfortable or needed to beat a hasty retreat: *poncho*. That was our mother's break-the-glass-in-case-of-emergency word she'd established halfway through her disastrous relationship with a menatally ill man thirty years her junior. We never learned if the code was inspired by stylish outerwear or a Mexican outlaw; in truth, we never asked. With Mom, we just never asked.

◡

After the ten-hour drive from the Baltimore airport to a suburb of Detroit, we were thrilled to be out of the car and ready to settle into our room at a Best Western. Ryan launched himself onto one of the queen-size beds, landing facedown with arms and legs outstretched. "Wake me up when it's time to eat," he said, voice muffled by a pillow.

I was in the bathroom washing off the road dirt and Maggie was hanging her "meeting the brothers" outfit in the closet when there was a knock on the door. I turned off the water and frowned. Maggie turned from the closet, her frown matching mine. "Who could that be?" she mouthed.

"How should I know?" I mouthed back.

A second, more insistent knock roused Ryan. He lifted his head, sleepy brown eyes taking in our inaction. "What's going on?"

The third knock was more pounding than knocking. I stepped to the door and peered through the peephole. A man. Cropped dark hair. Fiftyish. Repairman-type uniform. Maybe something was wrong with one of the motel systems?

Maggie looked at me with wide eyes, "Who is it?" she mouthed.

I flung my hands wide and looked back with my own wide eyes. "I don't know. A guy who works here, I think," I whispered.

She swatted at my hands as I reached for the door latch. "Don't open that if you don't know who it is!"

I angled my body to block her interference, confirmed the safety chain was on, then eased the door open. "Yes?"

"Hi. I'm David."

I blinked. Blinked again then turned and looked at Maggie, whose mouth hung open in disbelief. She'd made specific plans with David and Mike to meet them together in person for the first time at David's house tomorrow. "Um, just a minute," I said, then closed the door.

I did a Vanna White hand sweep from her to the door—a "you handle this" gesture.

She wagged her head. "What's he doing here?"

"Ask *him*!" I said, taking her by the shoulders and maneuvering her into door-opening position.

Ryan scrambled off the bed and struck a menacing pose: jaw jutted, fists balled, soccer-toned legs tensed for quick action. I gave Maggie's shoulders a squeeze of support while sending a mental cattle prod shock to David. What an arrogant asshole to show up without warning. To take Maggie by surprise. To take us all by surprise. I don't *like* being taken by surprise.

Maggie's hands shook as she released the safety chain. Though she'd talked to David on the phone dozens of times since their initial contact, this was the first time she'd experience him in the flesh. Her carefully planned reunion scenario—outfit, gifts, conversation, hugs—had been co-opted, as we learned later, by David's need to see her before anyone else did . . . especially their brother Mike.

David strode into the room like a cocky bantam rooster, radiating entitlement. I disliked him immediately. He laid out how the next couple of days were going to play out: where he was taking her, who'd she'd meet and when, and what his wife was cooking for breakfast, lunch, and dinner. There was no room for argument. I wanted to stab his overactive ego with a pitchfork. Ryan and I exchanged eye rolls during David's monologue, but Maggie seemed amenable, so into the chute we went.

A parade of Maggie's birth people marched through the next two days, showing her album after album of family photos, commenting on how much she favored her maternal grandmother, and sharing family stories. True to form, David dictated the schedule and micromanaged how every move and encounter should and would go.

On day three, Maggie said David was taking us further afield to meet extended family. "He's picking us up and. . . ."

I was suddenly pissed. Ripping pissed. I wasn't related to any of these people. I didn't want to meet any more strangers. Didn't want to look through any more photo albums. Didn't want to hear any more stories. My sister was no longer just *my* sister; she was David's and Mike's and was a half sister to at least three others. She was part of a biological tribe now, and though her birth family welcomed and embraced me, they weren't my tribe.

Maggie was floating. I was drowning. I really was happy for her, but each new introduction and exclamation felt like a sledgehammer. Wham—*you'll never know who you look like.* Wham—*you're still a shameful secret.* Wham—*you're not worthy of knowing.* I felt completely isolated. Singular. Unmoored.

"Sorry, not it. Not going. I can't take David one more minute."

"Well . . . what are you going to do?"

I knew exactly what I wanted to do. "I'm going to the lake house. Ryan, you want to go with?"

He brightened. "Yeah! We can get your $20 back!"

I laughed. The lake house was a modest home my maternal grandmother had built on the shore of Brendel Lake near Pontiac, Michigan. On our way to Detroit, I'd shared the story about how I'd sent a letter with $20 to the current owners asking them to buy a disposable camera and send me pictures. Never heard a peep from them in all these years.

∼

David's house was less than an hour away from the lake house. I'd spent the first five years of my life there, and summered there another three years after my dad's work took us first to South Bend, Indiana, then Indianapolis, then a momentary stop in Rockford, Illinois, and finally back to South Bend, where I'd lived until I was eighteen.

I'd loved the lake house. From my earliest recollections, I felt safe there. Even when I ran down the long slope to the lake, my body teetering on the brink of stumbling and rolling like a bowling ball over the seawall and into the water, I felt free and safe. I knew that lake, knew it would support me, both literally and figuratively. The seaweed and fish and lily pads would nurture me. Snails and pebbles and the pleated sand tinged green by the clear cold water—a comfy bed welcoming me. The water—a baptismal font, purifying me, cleansing me, buoying me.

~

In 1996, as my fortieth birthday loomed, I'd reflected on the lake house's importance to me. I wanted a memento from the house to help anchor me to the feeling of safety in those early years, so I wrote the following note and addressed it "To the current occupants":

Hello,

You don't know me, but I lived in your house from the mid-50's to the mid-60's. I'm coming up on one of those landmark birthdays, and have been reflecting upon my life. I spent the very happiest years of my childhood in "the lake house." My grandmother had it built. I teethed on the hearth. I loved running down the hill so fast that it took my breath away. I fished off the seawall.

I made a trip to Detroit last year and talked my father into making a side trip to see the lake house. I was overwhelmed with emotion at being in the neighborhood and seeing the house. I so wanted to knock on the door and ask to look around, but my dad was appalled by the notion, and so I settled for going over to the beach and gazing from afar. My contemplation was cut short by my impatient father—I think he thought we'd be fingered as trespassers or burglars casing the joint!

So where is this going, you ask? I know that one can

never really go home again, but it would be wonderful if you would send me some pictures of the house and yard. That is a lot for a perfect stranger to ask, but I have the strongest urge to connect to that house, or more likely, the happiness I felt when it was my home.

I have enclosed $20 to cover the expense of buying and mailing to me a disposable camera with which to take the pictures. Pardon my presumptuousness—I would completely understand if this is too weird a request to fulfill. But you would have my unending gratitude if you did this for me.

I don't know if anyone would still be around who would remember the Coopers, but you could ask around if you are uncomfortable about me being a potential thief! Anyway, thank you for considering my request. I hope you are as happy in your home as I was.

Best wishes,
Candi (Cooper) Byrne


I affixed a Curious George postage stamp to the envelope, rubber-stamped "Home is where your story begins. . . ." on the flap, and sent it off, certain that the current inhabitants would be moved by my heartfelt missive . . . or at least the $20.

Fourteen years later, I was still waiting for a response. Or at least my $20 back.

~

I turned at the weathered wooden sign that read BRENDEL HEIGHTS. I waited for a hallelujah-I'm-home feeling, but nothing surfaced as it had when Dad and I lurked here years before. Ryan and I bumped

along the unimproved tree-lined road, and I was struck by how familiar the drive felt—my secluded mountain home in West Virginia was
reached via a similar route. Stones popping, dust churning, wild ung-
roomed forest—the road Home.

We angled left and entered into a tamer landscape. I caught a
glimpse of the lake to my right and finally felt a rush of excitement.
*It's close! I know we're close!* We passed several massive contemporary
dwellings hogging the shoreline, completely out of place among the
modest vintage cottages and ramblers that had once had an unobstructed view of the lake.

"Greedy bastards," I mumbled. "Stealing the view from people
who've lived here sixty or more years. Hope that's not the kind of
people living in the lake house."

Ryan squinted in angry sympathy and nodded. "Yeah, greedy
bastards."

I pulled into a small, graveled parking area one house away from
533 Millwood—the lake house. Memories flowed. "See that house
there?" I said, pointing to the rambling two-story next to the lake
house. "Belonged to Mr. Frank. I used to hang out in his garage
while he was doing projects at his workbench. He had a collection
of Michigan license plates nailed to the wall. I used to do flips on his
porch railings."

The black iron railings had been replaced with non-flippable
rustproof ones. The garage now boasted a windowless door that likely
could be raised with a click of a button. It certainly didn't have the
character of Mr. Frank's cranky coils that complained loudly each
time he'd muscled open the heavy wooden plank.

A sign on the chain-link fence at the beach-access entrance next
to Mr. Frank's property sternly warned against trespassing, just as it
had when I was a kid. My parents never paid the beach-access dues,

so my brother and I were forced to navigate Mr. Frank's fenced sea-wall, jamming fingers into the small mesh as we slid tender feet along the rough rock lip pouting out from under the fence. We'd jump from the four-foot-high edge down onto the beach. At the end of the day, we'd stroll out through the access gate like we owned the place.

I tried the gate and found it unlocked. We walked over scrubby grass, then onto sand. It was early in the season, so the floating dock was beached. "I used to swim out to the dock and hide out under-neath with the fifty-five-gallon drums banging together from the wake of boats towing skiers," I said to Ryan.

Twin silver arcs dozed under a blue tarp. "I used to balance on top of that ladder—or one just like it—then jump off into the water. It was our version of a high dive."

I glanced around the beach, seeing it through Ryan's eyes. It was thirty-feet wide at best, the area more dirt and grass than sand. "They used to bring in dump trucks of sand every summer," I told him. "Your grandpa would help them rake it smooth."

He lifted his chin in acknowledgment.

*He's such a cool kid*, I thought. *No judgment from him. No questions. Just letting me have my moment.*

I walked to the edge of the shore. "There used to be a clear stream here . . . more of a trickle, really. The water was cold and there was a pathway of tiny pebbles along the bottom. Light blue flowers—fairy flowers, I used to think—grew along the stream. I would pick them and watch them float along into the lake."

Looking down at the water's edge I continued my soliloquy. "There were always millions of minnows. I tried catching them, but they were too fast for little fingers to grab hold."

I'd suffered from migraines in my mid-twenties and experi-enced a series of ministrokes that left holes in my memory. Even now, memories disappear into those potholes, but somehow, lake-house memories remained fully intact and visceral.

I could smell the baby oil my mother would doctor with iodine to create a self-tanning suntan lotion; the bastings likely caused the skin cancer that would later require drastic treatments to remove.

I could feel the dimples made by my preschool fingers poking into the grainy concrete frosting my dad spread across the top of our seawall.

I could hear the burr of the telephone ringing inside the black metal casing my mother had installed on the willow tree at the water's edge. She didn't want to miss the call from the adoption agency about their impending third child—my sister, Maggie.

A thunking sound interrupted the cascade of memories. I looked around and saw a man tossing wood chunks into a pile . . . in my yard! "Excuse me," I yodeled through cupped hands, "do you own the house?"

He lifted his head and searched me out. "Huh?"

"Do you own the house?" I repeated.

"I live here."

"I used to live there too!"

He scratched his head. "Did you send a letter a few years back?"

Ryan and I looked at each other, eyes wide, grinning. I turned back and said, "Why yes, I did!"

"My mom will definitely want to talk to you," Woodchucker said.

"And we want to talk to her about—" Ryan tapped the back of one hand against the palm of the other, talking from the side of his mouth, "Mr. Andrew Jackson."

Ryan and I went out through the beach gate, crunched through the gravel of the small parking lot, and trooped past Mr. Frank's garage and onto the large slab of concrete that covered the entire front yard of the lake house.

Up close, I could see the paint on the house was dull and chalky. The low cement stoop had pulled away from the house, canted and cracked from eighty years of Michigan winters. Tight fingers of green-and-white-striped hosta reached through the earth along the foundation, several weeks away from unfurling into soft mounds as they had every year since my grandmother had planted them when the house was built in 1935. My mother had transplanted slips of those hosta—daughters of those hosta—into the earth along the foundation of each of the dozen houses we'd lived in, literally grounding her roots as we moved from one house to the next in the nomadic life necessitated by my dad's burgeoning computer-programming career.

After Mom died, I excised a fistful of hosta from the front of her house. I wrapped the roots in a wet paper towel, then tucked them into a Ziploc bag. By the time I traveled from South Bend to West Virginia, the plants were looking wilted and slimy. I hospitalized them in a small planter filled with organic soil. They perked up within two days, but before I could get them into permanent ground, deer browsed the leaves to the soil line, then came back the next day to finish off the roots.

As I looked at the row of hosta my grandmother had planted, I briefly considered asking the homeowner if she'd let me dig up a hunk. *She wouldn't even send me pictures; unlikely she'd be open to me violating her vegetation.*

Ryan and I stood at the door, the threshold I'd crossed thousands of times. What was it like for my parents having gone out this portal as a barren, childless couple and returning hours later with me, a six-week-old infant born of an unwed mother? Did they feel gratitude toward the teen? Did they ever want to meet her? Size her up? Take a gander at my genetic future? How is it I'd never asked them these questions? How is it I had never thought about these questions until standing on an uneven stoop getting emotional over perennials?

"Gonna knock?" Ryan asked, pulling me from my reverie.

Woodchucker's mother welcomed me into my former home and gestured toward the dinette in the kitchen breakfast nook. She was in her early seventies, plump beneath her well-worn housecoat. Gray hair was corralled on bristled rollers, skewered into place with pink plastic picks.

"Please sit," she said, her words delivered with a slight whistle due to her lack of front teeth. She was immediately apologetic about not having responded to my note of oh so many years ago. "Still have the letter," she said. "Still has the $20 in it too, though there was times that money woulda come in real handy." She dispatched Woodchucker to fetch the letter from her bedroom.

He must have known exactly where she kept it, because he was back within a minute bearing the envelope with my familiar handwriting. After an impatient "well g'wan and give it to her" gesture from his mother, he slid it across the table to me. "Yeah . . . mighty handy, but it weren't mine to spend, leas' not on myself."

I glanced around the room; to my memory, it was almost exactly the same as it was in 1964, the last time I'd been in the house. One notable exception: an expanse of knotty pine cabinets with wrought iron handles and hinges had been sacrificed to create a view of the lake from the nook. I complimented the decision to do that.

"My husband did that right after we bought the place."

"When was that?" I asked.

"Don't remember the 'zack year. Prolly '64 or '65 . . . sometime round there."

I blinked in surprise. "Oh . . . well, then, you must have bought it from my parents."

She slid a finger under a curler and scratched her scalp. "Was a real pretty blonde lady," she said. "Real pretty and real nice." Ryan and I looked at each other with raised eyebrows. Mom? Real pretty, yes. Real nice . . . uh, no. "My mother was Delphine Cooper—"

"Yeah! Cooper . . . that was her. She let me and my husband move in early." The homeowner patted her crown of thorns. "We was having some trouble with the bank, and she let us stay here for a couple of weeks before the paperwork got all settled. Didn't charge us a penny." Ryan and I gaped in unison. "Nice" was hard enough to believe, but Mom letting strangers camp for free was unfathomable. I'd never experienced that Delphine Cooper.

I asked the woman if I might look around the house. She shifted uncomfortably, then said she was embarrassed by the condition of her home and couldn't bear for me to see beyond the kitchen. "Would you consider letting me take a picture of the fireplace? I literally cut my teeth on the hearth," I said. "There may be tooth marks there even now."

She looked puzzled by the request, then nodded. "Guess it's the leas' I can do seein's how I kept your money all these years."

She followed me around the corner into the front room. The fireplace dominated the north wall and was just as I'd remembered it—long rectangular slabs of deckle-edged stone in shades of butterscotch, caramel, and cream. The firebox was curtained by the same folds of dark chain mail I'd drawn open and closed like a theater drape as I'd strutted and danced on toddler legs along the hearth, a smooth gray expanse of slate. Tears welled as I gazed upon this safe and solid anchor of the happy times before Mom and Dad drank, before Mom's *Valley of the Dolls* years and bottomless prescriptions, before Mom's cosmetic surgery addiction—a reaction, I was sure, to Dad's lifelong philandering.

Mom had been happy in this house, the house that her mother had built and adorned with hosta, the house that had been Mom's home for almost thirty years. Suddenly, I could imagine the compassionate Delphine who'd dwelt in this home allowing a young couple with bank-paperwork problems to take up residence without her charging a penny.

I was seized by an overwhelming desire . . . the *need* . . . to buy this house. I was significantly underemployed, and my savings amounted to the $20 the homeowner had just returned to me, but I wanted this safe and happy home back. I yearned for the legacy of this lake house. I wanted my children and grandchildren to run down its hill, fish off the seawall, and chase minnows as I had. To know it, imprint on it, and elevate it to a destination of choice.

I wanted the fantasy of being the beloved daughter of a happy Delphine and the "Rock of Gibraltar" she'd always claimed my father to be . . . until he wasn't. Reality: They both had gotten lost inside bottles, and Little Candy was fast-tracked and promoted to Little Mother, who then made big mistakes and later spent decades trying to find the way back to that little girl interrupted.

A text message buzzed, real life shattering the fantasy of reclaiming the house. "Where R U?! BBQ w/fam @4:30!!!!!!"

I looked toward Ryan, who'd been standing silent sentry at the front-room doorway, and waggled the phone. "Your mom. We've got to hit the road." His wordless nod said, *Ready when you are.*

He turned to me once we were out of sight of the house and offered up a high five, his eyes flashing with devilish glee. "Score! We got your $20 back."

# Chapter 6

Pacing the deck overlooking the acres of trees in spring bud surrounding my West Virginia home, I dialed my sister then regaled her with the story of Aunt Dolores's vision the evening before; the miraculous discovery of my birth mother's identity; and the decision to head to Michigan for answers. Because I'd supported her five years earlier through her reunion, I wanted the same—expected the same—from her now that it was my turn for connecting with birth folk.

She'd been somewhat supportive during the early times of my frustration around my birth mother's denying me contact. After meeting her birth family though, she stuck with the story that I was better off not having contact. "But I don't want contact; I just want information," I'd said again and again. I was only making contact now because Mary had left me no other choice; I had no intention of maintaining a relationship. Get the answers and get out.

"Look what happened to me . . . all that those stupid men wanted to do was talk about themselves. They never asked anything about me," she said. "They keep calling and texting; why don't they get the hint that I don't want to talk to them?!"

Deep breaths. "Why don't you just tell them how you feel and be done with it?"

"They are just so stupid and selfish to make it all about them. You're really better off not being in touch."

*Ack—easy for you to say now that you're on the other side of know-ing your people and where you come from and who you look like!*

"I can't just get up and go tomorrow," she said. "Besides, this is way too soon." Maggie's refusal to accompany me on my impulsive trip shouldn't have surprised me, but it did.

"Way too soon? Maggie, I've been trying to get information about and from her for six years! How much longer do you think I need to wait?!"

"I don't know . . . but going tomorrow. . . ." She trailed off.

"Yeah?"

"Well . . . it's too fast. I waited a couple of months before meeting those stupid boys, and—"

I silently screamed, then cut her off. "Okay. Fine. Never. Mind."

"So, you're not going to go." Declarative.

"Of *course* I'm going to go! It was a fucking miracle—I'm not *not* going to go where I was divinely led!"

~

Standing on my birth mother's stoop—the very place I'd adamantly declared for years I'd never set foot—knuckles tingling from the knock on her door, a thought rose: *Why now, Universe? Why now, and why this way? Why Aunt Delores's vision? Why the miracle of finding Mary's name and address?*

*Mom,* a distant corner of my mind answered. *Mom has some-thing to do with this.* I cast a sidelong glance toward the sky and held my hands palms up in silent question to my dead mother.

*Mom?*

Mom didn't answer.

Neither did Mary.

I flexed my fingers. Tugged down the hem of my blouse. Wiped my sweaty palms along the side seams of my denim capris.

*What's the deal here, Mom?*

I knocked again, hands now stinging from rapping on the windowless wooden door.

Flexed, tugged, wiped. Shuffled foot to foot. Looked over my shoulder.

Snort giggled.

*Owa . . . mah . . . ghaaaad . . . this . . . is . . . hilarious. Mary's not home. What the hell, Mom?* I chuckled as I turned and went back down the stoop. Chortled as I got back in the car and drove off. Heehawed until I coughed so hard I couldn't see and pulled over on the main drag to recover.

I blotted my nose, then sipped from my water bottle. "Jesus, how anticlimactic." After years of drama and trauma and weeping and wailing and angst and anger and praying and therapy, after all the effort of prying my white-knuckled hands from the cosmic steering wheel to allow a miracle, after all the single-minded urgency of the past forty-eight hours . . . Mary. Wasn't. Home.

*Sooooo . . . what?* I went through possibilities. She was shopping and would be back soon. She was visiting her sister or friends and would be back soon. She was home and didn't open the door to strangers, even to one who might look like a younger version of herself. She was home and didn't open the door to strangers, especially to one who looks like the guy who impregnated her almost sixty years earlier. She was in a casket at the local funeral home, having died at the precise moment I'd found her mother's obituary.

*Get a grip, Byrne.*

I fished through my purse for my phone. *I'll call her. What am*

*I gonna say if she answers? What am I gonna say if I have to leave a message? Should I leave a message? Wouldn't it be weird if I didn't? She must have caller ID, right? She'd see my number, but no message . . . might freak her out. No doubt it'll freak her out to get a message.* "Bwaaaaah—quit overthinking this!"

I consulted the printouts from the BeenVerified database. I tapped her number then with a front-of-the-roller-coaster gut tumble, I pecked the connect icon. After three rings, I heard her voice, light-hearted and almost musical, sharing her disappointment over having missed my call and her assurance she'd get back to me as soon as possible.

"Um, hi . . . there. This is . . . *Candi*," I said, trying to imbue my name with meaning. I hadn't determined if she lived alone, so couldn't leave a straightforward message for fear of outing her. "We have a friend in common, *Loretta Colton*? From *Catholic Charities*? I'm in Buchanan, and I'd really like to stop by and talk with you today." I repeated my phone number twice, then ended the call.

I slumped against the seat back. *Hooooollllly. Shit!*—I'd just heard the voice of the woman who'd given birth to me. Was my cellular structure morphing . . . dormant areas lighting up having heard the sound I'd listened to and felt vibrations from for nine months? I hadn't considered it before—had she talked to me, her tiny partner in crime . . . put her hands on her ripe belly and regaled me with stories, fantasies of how she wished our lives could be?

I shifted in the Toyota's bucket seat and lifted the water bottle for another sip. I paused, bottle in midair. Or had she spewed hateful thoughts toward her unwanted passenger, the lump of flesh who'd caused her to be cast away from her family. Shamed. Shunned. Sent to solitary confinement.

Or maybe she'd ignored her ballooning abdomen, stoically

enduring kicks and summersaults, abdicating feelings and attachments so that I became a thing, not a baby. Not her baby. Just a problem to get rid of and move on from. Given her unwillingness over the years to even entertain the idea of connecting with me, I'd put my money on door number three. Shut down. Shut it out. Shut up.

I looked around and noticed villagers had gathered on three porches, eyes trained on the emotional foreigner parked in their zone. Torches and pitchforks were no doubt being readied. Time to skedaddle.

I cruised her house once more, and aside from Mr. Wheel Horse having finished his meticulous mowing, nothing appeared to have changed in the twenty minutes since I'd stood on her threshold.

*Except for me.*

I'd changed. I'd done the hard thing . . . the hardest thing I'd ever done in my life was knocking on that door. My nervousness was gone. *For the moment.* "Yes, but it will never be that hard again."

I pulled onto the gravel shoulder in the shade of a big maple two houses away from hers, rolled down the windows, and shut off the car. *I'll just sit here until she calls or comes home or until the natives get restless.*

It didn't take long before the garage door of the house across the street rattled open and a woman about my age walked out carrying a toddler. "Ooow, it's such a nice day today, isn't it, Benjamin," she said. I smiled in their direction then donned earbuds. The comforting downbeat of Pharrell's song "Happy" that I'd had on constant repeat for the entire drive *bahmp bahmp bahmp*'d in my ears, drowning out the blathering woman.

She walked across the street and behind my car. I noticed in the rearview mirror she'd taken in the out-of-state license plate before entering the house I was parked in front of. I sighed. *Just a matter of time before she circles the wagons.*

Five minutes later, I saw her in my side mirror. She stopped at the rear door like a cop who'd pulled me over for a traffic violation. *Is she going to ask to see my license and registration?* I saw her lips moving. Pharrell was asking if I felt like I was a room without a roof, so I missed what Officer Busybody said. I pulled out my earbuds and twisted around to look at her. "Sorry?"

"Do you need any help?"

"No, thank you," I said, lifting the earbuds to plug back in.

"Because I noticed you just sitting here and saw you were from West Virginia and when I asked Stephanie," she gestured with her toddler-free hand toward her neighbor's house, "if she knew you, she said no, so I thought maybe you might need some help," she said without taking a breath.

*Shit—totally busted.*

"Nope. Just waiting for a phone call," I said, swinging the earbuds.

She shifted the toddler to the other hip and gave me a dubious look. "Are you here on business?"

*Well that's none of your business.* "I'm visiting family. In South Bend," I hastened to add.

One eyebrow rose to Spock level. "Why would anyone want to come from South Bend to *Buchanan*?"

*Think fast. Think fast.* "Uh . . . for the cranberry wine at the Round Barn Winery."

She blinked.

"Do you know it?" I asked.

"My best friend owns it," she said, her face inscrutable.

"Then I'm sure you've enjoyed their fabulous cranberry wine. I had them ship me three cases for my fiftieth birthday party. You know, even people who don't like fruit wine like that cranberry wine," I enthused. She frowned. *Tone it down, Byrne . . . you're overselling.* "Well, guess I'd better get back on the road," I said brightly.

She nodded in a "betcherass you'd better get back on the road" way. "Don't drink and drive. Or talk and drive," she said, looking at the earbuds meaningfully.

"No, ma'am. Moderation and hands-free, that's me." *Ferchrissakes, Byrne, shuuuut. Uuuup.*

She gave me a hairy eyeball for the road, then cooed at her squirming toddler. *Damn, won't be able to come back until it gets dark.* She went back through her garage and closed the drawbridge. I looked at the car clock: 2:05. *What the hell am I going to do for the next seven hours?* "Duh . . . cranberry wine."

～

The Round Barn Winery tasting room was open and oddly busy for three o'clock on a weekday. Couples and groups bellied up to the long bar, chatting and laughing. I felt conspicuous and pathetic as the sole solo; even the bartenders were working in pairs.

*The last time I was here was with Mom . . . and now I'm here killing time until I can meet my birth mother.* I don't recall why I'd been in South Bend, or what had possessed me to voluntarily spend time with Mom, but I do remember thinking she would like the winery, so I'd suggested an outing. I'd longed for fun mother-daughter time—easy and familiar talk about my kids, work, our shared memories—which would have been a first, but she'd slept corpse-like in the back seat for the thirty-minute drive. She popped to full alertness as I pulled into the parking lot, then got out of the car and racewalked to the tasting room.

By the time I'd gotten inside, she'd commandeered a stool at the bar and was already sipping a glass of something red. At the time, tastings were free, and she took full advantage, rapping her knuckles on the wooden bar top, signaling the bartender for another hit of syrupy wine. No need for variety; just keep the sweet stuff coming.

I felt embarrassed by her excess while at the same time envious of her utter disregard for convention. She was single-mindedly self-centered and took what she wanted when she wanted it. There was no question in her mind that she deserved it—she was royalty, and all were subordinate to her. Demand, receive. Simple.

As she drank, I'd studied her profile, the softness and wrinkles expected in a seventy-something woman erased by countless cosmetic surgeries. Her hairline looked as if it had been drawn with a ruler . . . and it very likely had. The last lift had left her forehead at high tide. Her doctor had harvested patches of hair from atop her head and then relocated them at her temples, creating a boxy, artificial hairline.

Mom was gaunt, bones and blood vessels in high relief beneath her skin. Her purchased breasts were the only sign of cushion on her body. False advertising though—whatever substance they'd injected to defy gravity had left her with hard Barbie boobs.

I took a deep breath to chase away the memory of that trip, tossed the Toyota keys on the bar, then perched uncomfortably on a barstool. I reflected—not for the first time—how Mom must have been embarrassed by my excess—ham-hock arms, bustle butt, and Buddha belly. I'd been a plump baby, chubby child, hefty teen and now, an obese adult.

Mom was larger than life; was my weight the only way I knew how to be larger than life? She never overtly shamed me for my size, but did try different tactics meant to reduce it. She put me on diet pills when I was in the third grade. Our family drug dealer, er, doctor, had prescribed speed. As I ping-ponged off the walls of the principal's office, amped on the amphetamines, Mom claimed ignorance about why I suddenly could not sit still in class and focus.

She attempted to buy me into a smaller size, offering to pay me to lose weight. If I lost any weight, it was accidental because I'd had no idea about nutrition, exercise, or restraint. Whatever her strategy though, the message was clear—you literally do not fit in this family.

Mom and Dad looked like Lucy and Ricky Ricardo, glamorous, attractive, and stylish. Mom was a former model and actress. Dad garnered meaningful glances from women until his death at age seventy-nine. My sister was short, cute, and designer-label conscious even at an early age. My brother, nicknamed "Kenner Bird" for his loooong legs, strutted and preened with his fellow swim teammates with their wide wingspans and hide-nothing Speedos. And then there'd been me—Dumpy, Clumsy, and Hugey . . . my personal dwarves.

At the bar, one of the tag-team wine slingers ambled over. "Just you?"

In more ways than one, honey.

~

My mother and I had a difficult and contentious relationship for most of my life. I planned to run away when I was nine years old—packed a blue plaid suitcase with ratty day-of-the-week underwear and second-hand volumes of Nancy Drew mysteries. I had no idea where I'd go; I just knew I needed to get away from Mom's unpredictable and explosive moods. I wanted a mommy like my friends had—homebodies who gave hugs, made dinner, and stitched honor beads onto Camp Fire Girl ceremonial vests.

"I'm going now," I said, the unwieldy suitcase banging against my legs as I struggled to get out the door.

"What's going to happen to her if you leave?" Mom said, pointing to my sister in the red canvas jumpy chair in the corner of the kitchen. I'd made sure to change Maggie's diaper and snap her into a clean yellow terry sleeper before closing the zipper on my suitcase. "You're her little mother."

I was Maggie's "little mother" from the time our mother placed my newly adopted six-week-old sister into my eight-year-old arms. I was fiercely protective of Maggie but powerless against Delphine the Duchess. Except when I could get my mother to smile. Those smiles were hard-won. Humor. Wit. Puns. Jokes. Sarcasm. Pratfalls. I would work the room like a headliner in Vegas, with an audience of one—one whose twitchy hand rested on a rage rheostat.

I looked at Maggie's round chipmunk cheeks and pudgy hands. Her mouth split into a grin as she blew a series of slobbery raspberries and rose onto terrycloth-covered toes. Mom lit a Salem, then leaned against the kitchen counter. "We got her because *you* wanted her."

*What* would *happen to her?* Mom drew on her Salem, eyes narrowed. The haze of cigarette smoke wrestled with the sunlight streaming through the kitchen windows. Maggie banged the tray of the jumpy chair and crowed with glee. I tugged the suitcase back through the door to unpack, shame blanketing me. What was wrong with me that I could be so selfish leaving my baby unprotected.

~

We moved near Indianapolis in 1966 for yet another job change for my dad. It was a three-bedroom, one-and-a-half-bath rambler indistinguishable from the hundreds of other tract homes in the close-in Indy suburb. My parents had the master bedroom, my brother, one of the two smaller bedrooms, my sister, the other. My sleeping area was in the windowless mudroom between the kitchen and attached garage.

I sat on the edge of my twin bed fingering the trim on the low bookcase that doubled as a nightstand and unintentional doorstop for the door to the attached garage. Both door and bookcase regularly exchanged insults—white paint on the corner of the bookcase, brown freckles on the door. The door was temperature controlled— that is, freezing in the winter, scorching in the summer. Noxious petroleum and chemical smells permeated the uninsulated wall boards and seeped into my alcove. I felt like Cinderella—cooking, cleaning, washing, taking care of my eighteen-month-old sister and eight-year-old brother. I was ten.

On this day, lunchtime was on the horizon and there was no food in the house. Nothing in the wheezy fridge except a pitcher of bilious green Kool-Aid. Nothing in the freezer save for moody ice trays and a frost-enrobed bottle of vodka. The kitchen cupboard shelves held a half dozen tins of McCormick spices, a blue cardboard canister of Morton salt, a can of Crisco shortening, and a half bag of Domino sugar.

I'd mentioned to Mom the day before that we needed groceries. She'd been sitting on the couch, her legs crossed and partially curtained behind a striped cotton shirtwaist dress. Rope-soled canvas slides revealed peasant feet; the red polished nails were not enough to overcome the evidence of generations of hard field work.

She lifted a tumbler of Mogen David wine to her lips, then a Salem. I scanned for signs of impending eruptions. Her hands were relaxed, her brow smooth. She sipped at her cigarette, the tip barely reddening. No . . . no immediate danger. She was off somewhere. *I'll let her be for a while and mention it again later.*

Now I wished I'd pressed the issue yesterday, because I had no idea what to do about the mom who'd been sitting in the garage for hours. It was almost noon, and I knew Peter would blow in hungry after a morning of playing Army in the backyard. Without even Crisco-and-sugar sandwiches as an option—I'd used the last of the spongy Wonder Bread and the sole egg to make French toast for breakfast—I had to do something soon.

Ghostly fingers of cigarette smoke fluttered through the gap where I'd left the door to the garage slightly ajar. Mom was quiet. Scary quiet. Hair-trigger quiet. I worried the chenille bedspread, seeking and tugging at loose nap.

From the vantage point in my sleeping alcove, I could see Maggie systematically transferring gnawed wooden blocks one by one from the front room to her hidey-hole under the kitchen table. I sucked air through my teeth each time she ducked to clear the silver metal hem of the Formica-topped table, certain she'd whack her head. Maggie would be hungry soon too.

Options. What were the options to get food for these kids? I knew my dad worked with big computers at IBM, but I didn't know where that was, even though he'd take me to work occasionally on Saturday mornings. He'd give me manila cards he said I could practice my penmanship on. The cards had rows of numbers in teeny print on one side, but the backs were blank. The nib of my fountain pen four-wheeled over the lace of rectangular holes left in the aftermath of the cards being punched. Dad said the computer read the holes, but he had to be kidding; machines couldn't *read*.

I knew we had money to buy food because Mom had me keep the checkbook and pay the bills. She'd shown me how to slice open the bills with a steak knife, note the amount and due date on the front of the envelope, then write out the checks and track them in the check register.

I'd been in charge of grocery shopping for months. I was out-wardly casual but secretly thrilled by the attention of the cashiers and other shoppers as I navigated the aisles of the A&P with Maggie in the cart, shopping list penned on a punch card clutched tightly in my hand along with the red vinyl-covered checkbook. Mom parked our Fairlane station wagon in the loading zone and chain-smoked until I finished shopping.

I thought about riding my bike to the store. Peter could stay behind and play with his platoon, but I couldn't leave Maggie . . . not with the storm brewing in the garage. I peeled away a sliver of thumbnail with my teeth as I contemplated other options. I quickly dismissed the idea of asking the neighbors for food or a ride—they'd ask too many questions.

From outside, I heard Peter and his squad *bbbrraahh*ing as they aimed and fired plastic weapons. In the kitchen, Maggie patiently tried taming the chairs that were rearing on hind legs. No other option left but to ask Mom. I took a deep breath and stood, sweaty feet squelching in filthy Keds. I put my hand on the knob and eased the door fully open.

The garage was choked with cigarette smoke. Through the haze, I could see Mom sitting in an aluminum lawn chair. She looked like an evil queen—unyielding erect posture, hair sculpted into a lacquered bun crowning her head, and a glowing Salem scepter angled between two fingers. "Mom?" I ventured timidly. Her face remained in profile.

Smoke stung my eyes, and I blinked hard against the protective tears. From behind me, in the safety of her kitchen-table fort, Maggie squealed with delight as tumbled blocks chimed and pinged against the table and chair legs. In the backyard, little-boy voices volleyed— the words muted by distance, but the intent clear: "Ours!"; "No, ours!"

I tried again. "Mom? Um . . . there's nothing here to fix for lunch." My stomach felt hot and tight as I waited for her to respond. My toes clenched and scrubbed against the slimy insoles of my shoes.

The silence was thick and unbearable.

"Mom, we need to go to the groc—"

She ejected from the chair. It clattered backward and collapsed. Her forehead and chin compressed her face into a fist of rage. She plowed through the doorway bellowing, "What about the God. Damn. *Carrots!*"

*My mommy is a monster.* I stumbled out of her path, my feet skidding in the swampy Keds. I lost my balance and hit my head on the sharp corner of the bookcase. Blood flooded my eye from a wide gash in my right eyebrow, poured down my face, dripped onto my lips, and spattered the front of my T-shirt. I gasped as pain hammered my head.

I heard a crash. *Maggie? Hurt?* I swiped at my bloody mask with the bedspread, the nubby chenille abrading the wound. Two thuds sounded from the back of the house. Grabbing a shirt from the floor, I pressed it against my brow to staunch the bleeding and wobbled into the kitchen.

I blinked and squinted and bent down to look under the kitchen table for Maggie. She seemed completely unfazed by the noise and my bloody state. *Safe. She's safe. Where's Peter?* I lifted the shirt away from my eye long enough to see into the backyard, where he and his friends were trooping into their Army base, a red wooden playhouse left behind by the previous owners.

*Thud. Thud. Thud.*

I heel-toed silently out of the kitchen and down the hall. I peered around the laundry-room door and saw the floor littered with tin cans and my mother fishing in the cupboard over the washer and dryer. She whirled on me, brandishing a can in each hand. The white labels with black block print were devoid of color or brand name. Mom had scored cases of the dented cans from the Railroad Surplus

Store for a dollar. The contents, I knew all too well, consisted of carrot coins whose color and flavor had been leeched out by the industrial canning process, leaving only flaccid yellow disks. The mere thought of ingesting the contents of the institutional-pack cans triggered my gag reflex.

"There. Are. God. Damn. *Carrots* to eat," she growled, thrusting the cans out at arm's length, shaking them like maracas.

The memory goes dark at that point. I imagine I did feed the kids those goddamn carrots, then slipped them candy from my stash. *Sugar makes it all better, little ones.* I regularly pilfered a one-pound bag of plain M&Ms from the A&P, and sweated discovery of my theft until I could slide the contraband under my mattress. Mom had her pills; I had mine.

Neither parent ever acknowledged the bruise on my forehead, nor the half-inch gash in my eyebrow that took months to heal. To this day, the lumpy scar makes it appear as if I am terminally inept at plucking.

∼

One summer afternoon when I was thirteen years old, I blew out of the front door, fuming over Mom's decree that I couldn't go to the local swimming hole with friends because "Your sister needs you; you're her little mother." That had worked once, but it was not going to work again. "I'm not a little mother," I'd shouted, "I'm a *kid*," and I took off for Pinhook Lagoon on my blue single-speed Schwinn, about ten miles from our new home in South Bend.

After an afternoon of swimming and lolling with my pals in Pinhook's strip of weed-stubbled sand, I didn't want to return home to the adult responsibilities waiting for my young shoulders to bear. It seemed like a fine idea, then, to accept a ride from two strangers who'd suggested I ditch my bike and cruise around with them in a souped-up Chevy.

They later dumped me on the side of the road, miles from my bike and home. I slept in the grass behind a nearby hotel, then walked home in the morning, a paste of semen mixed with blood chafing my bruised thighs. I so needed a mommy at that moment, someone to tend to me, comfort me, threaten grievous bodily harm to the men who'd sprayed their biological graffiti on my virginal walls and then discarded me like a spent beer bottle.

Hand on the square brown porch pillar for support, I winced and groaned as I lifted one achy, shaky leg then the other onto the wide concrete porch slab. I shambled to the front entrance of our house, a set of doors, the bottom halves made of heavy wood, the top halves a series of paned glass. I stepped up onto the narrow Chicago-brick stoop, hand on the shiny brass doorknob, and pushed the right-hand door open.

Except it didn't open. My shoulder thudded against the wooden frame, sending waves of pain down my body to meet the relentless crests of pain rising from below. I teetered on the edge of the brick, forced backward by the momentum, saved from a fall to the concrete by my hand gripping the doorknob.

I tried the knob again, twisting my hand right, then left to no avail. I dropped my head and whimpered. I needed to be inside. I needed a shower. Sleep. I needed to be cocooned and swaddled. I needed to have someone make it all better. Make it all go away. I jiggled the handle and twisted again. I finally registered that the door was locked. We *never* locked the door. *Why is the door locked?* Brow furrowed, I tapped a knuckle on the doorframe.

My mother strode into view, her usually bunned and sculpted blonde hair limp and untamed. Jaw clenched, shoulders folded forward, she glared at me through the door. I felt tears welling. My legs quaked from a combination of fear, pain, and exhaustion. "Mom?" It came out a choked croak. I coughed and tried again. "Mom?"

Silence. Moments ticked by, the heat of her fury scorching my tender, wounded soul.

"Mom . . . Mom . . . Mom," I hiccuped plaintively.

Silence.

Tears streaming, snot fauceting, I begged, "Mom . . . please let me in. Pleeeeease let me in. Mom . . . please." My voice trailed off into a whispered chant, "Pleasemomletmeinpleasemomletmeinplease momletmein. . . ."

Wordlessly, she turned and walked away, leaving a nearly catatonic me to marinate on the front porch. An hour later, my dad's silver Thunderbird barreled up the driveway; Mom had obviously called him home from work. He stepped around me without a word, then rattled the front door. Mom let him in, then snicked the lock back on.

Five minutes later, he was back on the porch rolling up the cuffs of the white dress shirt I'd starched and ironed the morning before. Mom watched through the front door as Dad wailed on me with a three-inch-wide razor strop until the leather handles flew off.

～

When I was sixteen, my mother ordered my boyfriend, Brendan, off our property during a pool party with my friends and pizza-parlor coworkers. "What is *he* doing here?" she snarled at me. "Get out," she barked at him, her arm extended, pointing toward the driveway. His eyes narrowed and his mouth tightened; I silently willed him to stand up to her. *Fight! Fight for me! Fight for us!* Instead, he made his way up the pool ladder and out to his car, soggy footprints trailing behind him. I heard his Opel Kadett start up, then the noise of his engine fading as he drove away.

My friends scrambled out of the pool; wordlessly claimed their towels, clothes, and keys; and sloshed to their vehicles. Car doors slammed, engines revved, and tires squealed as they beat a retreat from Delphine the Dragon Lady. I followed her into the front room. She settled into her throne—one of a pair of love seats flanking the fireplace. I could smell the chlorine from the water puddling at my feet as I confronted her: "How could you do that to me? It was humiliating."

She took a drag of her Virginia Slim and crossed her legs, unfazed. The pendulum of the Regulator clock in the family room *ticktock*ed the passing moments. The cigarette glowed and dimmed as she raised it to her lips, then lowered her arm to rest on the end table.

"Well?" I shrieked, frustrated and angered by her silence. She turned her head toward me and took inventory—my shaggy sun-streaked hair, fleshy body, the dark amoeba of water around my feet staining the industrial beige carpet. The cigarette arced up to her mouth, then down again. "I don't like him and I don't want him here," she said finally.

"Well I do!"

"As long as you live here, what I say goes," she said.

I stormed and raged, but there were no further words from her. She lit another cigarette, then flapped open the newspaper, dismissing me. I packed that night and moved out the next day to live with one of my pizza-parlor coworkers. I'd left a note saying where I'd gone. Only later did I find out my mother destroyed the note before anyone else saw it, leaving my father, brother, and sister to worry for months about my whereabouts and well-being.

~

Much to my mother's consternation, at age eighteen, I married Brendan, the banished boyfriend, and moved from South Bend to southern Maryland where he was stationed with the Navy. I bore our son, Kelly, eighteen months later, and our daughter, Caity, five years after that. In the interim, my dad had taken up with Jane, a clone of a thirty-years-younger Delphine—blonde, beautiful, and eccentric; Mom and Jane even wore the same heavy Youth Dew perfume. After I allowed my dad to visit with Jane, now his second wife—also referred to as the "bitch pig whore" by my mother—Mom refused contact with me for years. She marked an envelope I'd mailed to her with pictures of my children—her first grandchildren—"Deceased, Return to Sender," written in her distinctive handwriting with a thick black marker.

That feeling of rejection and abandonment echoed what I'd felt while begging my mother to let me in after the rape. Amplified it, because this time, it was clear she'd closed and locked the maternal door for good. Years of holidays, birthdays, and Mother's Days passed by without a word from her. I sent cards and gifts, and while none were returned, none were acknowledged. The phone calls and messages I left saying that Brendan, the kids, and I were in town went unanswered and unreturned. I'd been found guilty of treason against her and sentenced to solitary confinement as punishment.

~

I don't recall the circumstances under which we finally achieved détente, but at some point in my forties, Mom and I reconnected, if only superficially. I'd undergone a smorgasbord of therapy and other forms of how-to-un-fuck-up my life in the run-up to, and through, my divorce from Brendan, two decades after he'd been summarily ejected from the pool party.

Mom still had the power to trigger me though. Shame burns hot when I think of how I screamed at her in the lobby of the Hampton Inn the night before my son's wedding. I was incensed that while she could afford to travel to exotic destinations for months at a time, she refused to ante up for her own hotel room. I unleashed my inner harridan and hurled invective without regard for the shocked onlookers. Mom turned from me, took out her credit card, and accepted a room key, all without a word. I watched her struggle with her small carry-on case and purse, then shuffle out of the lobby.

In that moment, I'd felt triumphant: *How does* that *feel, Delphine?* Later that evening, I was horrified that I could so easily drop into a place of retribution. I wasn't Delphine . . . wasn't anything like her . . . except in that moment of public shrewery, I was. And I knew that to the outside world, I looked like a big fat raving maniac bitch heaping abuse upon a frail septuagenarian who didn't know how to defend herself. *She's the ice-hearted bitch, people! I'm the victim here!*

# Chapter 7

Two glasses of cranberry wine and years of difficult memories later, I was back in the car, with hours to go until I could once again troll Mary's house under the cover of darkness, out of nose-shot of her prying neighbors. *Eat? Not hungry. See a movie? Enh. Call everyone who's blowing up my phone asking for updates? Not till there's something to say.* I consulted the Rand McNally map book. "Well lookey here . . . big water."

Fifteen minutes later, I pulled into a deserted public-access parking lot for Lake Michigan. Two weeks from now, the place would be wall-to-wall trucksters packed with families who would crisp and burn after a day in the early summer sun. Happy families making and capturing memories . . . Facebooking and Instagramming shots of sandcastles, boogie-boarding, and aggressive gulls poaching snacks from the hands of toddlers.

It was about ten degrees too hot to consider walking the sandy fringe, so I settled for lake gazing through the windshield. A slight chop created a spangled harlequin pattern on the lake's surface, the diamond shapes hinged with winky crystals. Wavelets tongued the shore like a kitten lapping cream. The elemental experience of earth, wind, sun, and water soothed me. The combination of wine, the lullaby of the lake, and the adrenal aftermath of my frenetic road trip and thwarted attempt to meet Mary doped me into a twilight state. Sometime later, a car door slammed and I startled from my torpor.

I checked my phone: 4:30. No call from Mary. Four and a half hours to go until I could resume my reconnoitering. *Why couldn't Aunt Delores have had her vision when the days were shorter?*

I watched some sort of large watercraft slowly slide along the horizon. 4:47. Impulsively, I scrolled through my phone contacts and pressed the call icon for my sister's birth brother, Mike.

Mike, an officer with the Detroit Fire Department, and I had developed an easy friendship in the four years since my sister had been in reunion with him and her other birth brother, David. David was eerily similar to our adoptive brother, Peter—snarky, confrontational, and arrogant—while Mike was easygoing, irreverent, and tenderhearted. My sister hadn't maintained contact with Mike, but I had.

The call went to voice mail. "Hey, it's Candi. I'm in Saint Joe, Michigan. Come over and hold my hand while I wait for my birth mother to call." Fifteen minutes later, the phone flashed Mike's name on the screen.

"Hey, you!" I said.

"Hey . . . how'd you know I was at the doctor?" he asked, his tone unnaturally serious.

"Doctor? What's wrong?" *Hurt in a fire? Heart attack?*

"Hemorrhoids," he said, and laughed. We cracked wise for several minutes about his unfortunate malady, then Mike asked, "What's going on with you?"

"Guess you didn't listen to my message, huh?" I gave him the *Reader's Digest* version of how I came to be parked at the Lake Michigan dunes. "So, get yourself a butt donut and get your sore ass over here."

Love to, can't. Blah blah. Kids. Blah blah. Work tomorrow. Blah blah. Need a sitz bath.

"Fine," I groused.

"Hey, why don't you stay at the cottage when you're done? You can relax and regroup." Mike had recently purchased a modest, rustic lakeside second home and often shared with me pictures and tales of lake living.

I don't stay with people—there's no isolation force field. In the anonymity of a hotel room, I can cry, binge eat, and talk to myself without limits. No need to chameleon. No obligations. No concerns about who pays for dinner, what to do with the used sheets and towels, and where they hide the spare roll of toilet paper.

"You're sweet to offer," I said noncommittally. I dodged several more versions of his invitation, then signed off with a promise to call him when I was on my way to the cottage. *At least* someone *wants to see me.*

The rest of the afternoon passed at the speed of a bill going through Congress. I got gas I didn't need. Squeegeed the windshield. Hung out at the library with the other homeless sorts. My phone bleeped at least every half hour—my sister texting for an update. *NFW. If you were here, you'd know what was going on, wouldn't you?*

At six o'clock, I snagged a table at a dive pizza joint several blocks from Mary's house. Cheap dark paneling off-gassed the sticky odor of thousands of meals and a former smoking section. The tables were made of a brown laminate that would likely survive the end-times. Chair seats were more duct tape than vinyl. I knew with certainty my iced tea would come in a dark amber plastic glass with a hint of industrial sanitizer.

I chatted briefly with the waitress about the merits of their spinach pizza. Opened and closed my journal at least a dozen times, never

making a mark. What was there to say? I was disheartened and anx-
ious in my holding pattern, circling this small town waiting to land
again on Mary's doorstep.

After dawdling until seven o'clock, I left with seven-eighths of
the pizza stashed in a flimsy white box. The sun appeared to be nailed
in the same position it was when I'd gone into the restaurant. I got
into the car, dropped the pizza box onto the passenger-side floor-
board, then slumped against the steering wheel. I rocked and rolled
my head and made guttural noises of despair.

*I've wasted so much time, money, and energy. It's never going to
get dark. She's never going to call. I should just go anyway. Pull right
in her driveway. Gab with the nosy neighbors. "Yeah, I'm her first kid.
She gave me up for adoption and has kept it a secret all these years.
In this day and age, I know, right? No, thanks, I'll just wait here. You
g'wan back in and finish polishing your night vision goggles."*

Enough. I grabbed my phone, scanned the list of previously
dialed calls, and pressed Mary's number. *Answer, damn it. I can't
sit another second waiting for this friggin' party to start.* Three rings,
then the machine. *She really does have such a sweet voice. And an
accent. Canadian?* "Hi, Mary, it's Candi again. Really hoping to talk
with you soon. Please call me." I enunciated my phone number twice,
then pressed the icon to end the call. "Not giving up, Mary," I said to
the blank face of the phone.

The phone squawked and blatted, sending my heart rate into
heavy cardio range. "Jumpy much?" I asked, after realizing the tones
were generated from the weather app.

Severe weather warning—thunderstorms and heavy downpours
expected; localized flooding possible. Probable tornado activity.
Residents are advised to take cover.

I leaned forward and looked up through the windshield. The sun was still stubbornly stuck in the same position. I started the car and eased into traffic behind a wide-hipped Ford Megavehicle. *I could just about take cover under his truck.*

At the intersection, I had a clear view of the western sky—it looked like the hull of a dark gray warship bearing down on the blue sky in the east. "Shee-it, that don't look good." I pulled over, then scrolled through the weather app to the time-lapse radar map. A wide band of red stuttered and advanced rapidly across Illinois. "Man, that's moving fast." Enough time for one last dash past her house, neighbors be dammed. *Anyway, they're probably all headed for their basements.* Safe space. Coleman lanterns and battery-operated weather-band radios. Scratchy wool Army blankets. Mason jars of garden goodies. Board games. Cards. Mommies and daddies protecting their families.

It hadn't happened that way when I was growing up, no matter how I'd longed for someone to make sure we were safe. Mom was fearless and unflappable in the face of natural disasters, boogeymen, and bad guys, but she wasn't protective. Her "Tornado coming? I don't care" attitude read to me as "I don't care about *you*."

The atmosphere had taken on a greenish cast—a harbinger of the approaching storms. *Ticktock, chiquita.* Two turns and I was once again on Mary's block. Leaves shimmied in a wave of wind. I squinted at her house. Lights shone through the open slats of her blinds. There was a red pickup in her driveway. *That can't be* her *truck. Who's there with her? Would she have listened to the messages with someone else there?*

I continued the now-familiar route to the end of the street and turned around. The sky was a steel hand reaching forward and pressing down. Tree limbs flexed and arched as a frowny-faced puffed-cheek cloud blew gusts of wind. Streetlights flashed on. *She'll have to take me in with this bad storm coming, right?*

I slowed as I neared her house. The blinds were now closed and the lights turned off. *Oh. Oh. OhmyGod . . . did I . . . scare her?* I pressed my hand to my mouth. *Of course she'd be scared, dodo head. She's sitting in the dark, wondering what to do now that her secret knows where she lives. Knows her phone number. Called her. Twice.*

The spicy tang of rain bathing warm pavement scratched at my nose through the open car window. I heard teams of angels bowling strikes in the distance. *I've scared her. How will I make this right?* Big drops of rain plopped on my windshield as I headed back toward South Bend. *Don't know how. But I will. Tomorrow.*

# Chapter 8

I hadn't considered until halfway through the ten-hour trip from my West Virginia home exactly where I would stay once I got close to the birth-mother ship, though I knew it would be in or around South Bend, Indiana. South Bend was home. Ish. Because of Dad's computer-programming career, we'd yo-yoed from city to city, house to house, always landing back in South Bend. It wasn't Home Sweet Home, but it was the place I was most familiar with. *Home. I came home to come home to Home. Home to myself.*

The mile markers along the Ohio Turnpike flashed past as I contemplated staying with my brother, Peter. The route to my birth mother's house would take me, literally, past his backyard. Though we were close growing up, our relationship hadn't survived into adulthood. We were polar opposites where politics and religion were concerned—the left hand did know what the right hand was doing, and there was virtually no middle ground where the hands could shake in agreement.

I had touchstones in South Bend—my ex-husband's brother, Terry, and his wife of over fifty years, Bunny; three-quarters of their offspring; and two additional generations that Terry and Bunny were raising. I'd known Terry and Bunny since I was sixteen years old, and though I was twenty years split from my ex, Brendan—now married to wife number three—my in-laws always spread a wing for me to tuck under. Authentically and automatically, no matter how long between connections. "Welcome. We love you," was implicit. "You divorced Brendan, not us," was explicit. No judgments. No need to explain long absences. Just open arms and open hearts.

I teared up thinking of the last time I'd seen Terry, at my mother's viewing, and Bunny, at Mom's funeral. My sister and I had been in South Bend a week, cocooned at the hospital willing our mother to die, and hadn't called anyone. Terry and Bunny had seen Mom's death notice in the *South Bend Tribune* and made plans to attend the services, even without knowing we were in town. The Byrne way— family of family—you represent.

After Mom's ghastly funeral service, Bunny, my sister Maggie, and I had met in the lobby of the Inn at Saint Mary's on the outskirts of South Bend. We condemned my brother's choice of fire and brimstone readings, then cried about our respective dead mothers. Bunny sat wrapped in her mother's full-length fur coat, the taupe silk lining embellished with a label whose red script read "Christine Duddy"— Bunny's mother's name, and Bunny's given name. "She promised she would never leave me," Bunny said, sniffling. "She was right—I see her face in mine every time I look in the mirror."

I so envied her. I yearned to look in a mirror and see the face of my mother—not Delphine's face, but of the woman who gave birth to me, and the woman who gave birth to her.

∾

Here I was again at the Inn at Saint Mary's, and again in a situation like I was at the winery, where memories of Mom were juxtaposed against the delayed encounter with my birth mother earlier in the day. Rain slapped against the hotel window, diluting the view of the lush grounds of Saint Mary's College next door. The Inn at Saint

Mary's anchored the northeast corner of the campus and was a field goal kick away from Notre Dame across the street. Lightning strobed through the towering mass of dark clouds like a celestial short circuit. "Epic . . . kinda Dorothy in the twister," I marveled as the storm raged on, newspapers, fast-food wrappers, and leaves swirling and spiraling in front of the hotel room's picture window like a real-life *Wizard of Oz* scene. "What . . . no flying cows?"

I flipped open the lid of my doggy box and tugged a slice of pizza loose. I momentarily considered fetching a hand towel to use as a bib, then decided against extricating myself from the comfy perch I'd fashioned from the padded armchair and bath towels I'd draped across the seat and back as a cootie barrier. God only knows what manner of effluvium lurked in the upholstery. "They should make hotel furniture out of sterilizable metal like they have in prisons," I opined to my slippered feet parked on the windowsill.

I took a bite of pizza and mused as I chewed, "You know what they say about people who talk to themselves, Byrne?"

*Hmmm . . . maybe that their sister refused to accompany them on the biggest quest of their life?* Anger flared and throbbed in me. *Why isn't my sister here with me? I spent hours . . . weeks . . . months supporting her through her search and reunion with her birth family. Never mind all the caretaking I did while she was little. I nurtured and tended to her as if I were her mother. I'd been a rodeo clown, distracting Mom, the enraged bull, from charging at and goring the helpless one—"Hey, Mom, over here, see me? Come and get me. Leave the baby alone, bitch."*

# Chapter 9

The year I turned fifty, I quit my six-figure job, sold my house, divested myself of virtually all my belongings, and bought a twenty-nine-foot Winnebago to fulfill my fantasy of driving around the country in a Minnie Winnie. I'd pictured myself spending the days meeting interesting people and seeing breathtaking sights, then writing about my adventures. In my secret heart, *Winnie, Vidi, Vici* dominated the *New York Times* best seller list. Kathy Bates would play me in the movie.

In reality, the Winnie became a rolling hermitage. I did see breathtaking sights, but I kept to myself, pondering for hours on end about existential questions. Who was I? Why had the things that had happened to me happened? What was my purpose? As months and miles went by, I consulted oracle cards, wore crystals, and immersed myself in esoteric studies in hopes of finding answers in the meta-physical realm. After a year on the road, hopscotching from place to place, I recognized I'd spent way too much time alone and in my head, and needed to ground myself and reenter society.

In February 2008, I hung up my Winnie keys and settled into a small town along the coast of Northern California, the Pacific Ocean in view on one side, redwood-studded mountains on the other. I reveled in daily walks along the abandoned logging road that paralleled the ocean shore and offered an unobstructed view of the sea. Looking north on clear days, I could see the edge of the continent curve like the proud breasts of a figurehead on the bow of a ship. Red-winged blackbirds trilled and squeaked as I passed the patch of plump sepia cattails peeking above emerald fronds. The dry, sweet scent of sea oats mingled with the briny smell of the ocean, which along with the chilled fragrance of eucalyptus, combined into a heady perfume.

The waves called to me—sometimes in quiet, sibilant whispers, other times as the musical chuckle of pebbles nudging and tumbling in the receding surf. Most often, the waves shouted and demanded my attention, thundering toward the shore like white-maned horses at full gallop.

Isak Dinesen said, "The cure for anything is salt water: sweat, tears, or the sea"; my daily perambulations usually encompassed all three. I'd pound along the old logging road, the ocean pounding at me, salt scrubbing away the emotional sediment that the existential questions and metaphysical practices hadn't been able to dissolve. The wind wiped tears away before my hands could. Tears of regret. Tears of anger. Tears of hope.

～

One day, after an extra-long walk accompanied by particularly tumultuous combers, I timbered onto my bed, licking the salt from my lips and mining sand from my hair. Several deep breaths later, I felt a tingling in my body. It started behind my navel and radiated out until my whole body was buzzing. I couldn't move—it was as if a huge hand were holding me down until I was filled with positive ballast. I felt an energy move through me, like a comet with a long tail. In its wake, I felt the enmity toward my mother vaporize. The loving-kindness prayer sprang to mind and I chanted countless rounds to my mother, filling the void, now empty of anger, hurt, and disconnection, with compassion, forgiveness, and love.

*May you be filled with loving-kindness.*
*May you be well.*
*May you feel peaceful and at ease.*
*And may you be happy.*

I awoke later, disoriented in the darkness. My lips burned from overexposure to the sun and wind. My nostrils felt dry and crinkly, like they'd been shrink-wrapped. My eyes were filled with enough grit to sand barnacles from the bottom of a boat.

My phone repeated a missed-message alert. *Glad something woke me up before I shriveled completely into jerky.* I tromboned the phone, squinting to see the display with debris-filled eyes. *Gonna drink a gallon of water. Then take a shower. Then check the message.* I smiled. *Then call Mom.* I shook my head, amazed . . . and . . . kinda freaked about the whole loving-kindness thing.

As the shower sluiced away the sea crust, I tried to make sense of what had happened that afternoon. How had decades of conflict with Mom resolved in an instant? What was that . . . buzzing-energy thing that had pumped loving-kindness into me? Had resuscitated me—out with the bad, in with the good. And why now?

An hour later, clean, refreshed, and rehydrated, I checked the phone and saw that it was my brother who'd called. *Peter? What does he want? I wonder if he's calling to brag again about how important he is to the school board. Or how busy he is, what with his important job and his important work as an athletic coach. Or maybe he's calling with another political screed about how important family values are . . . except when the family is on welfare or has gay parents. Ugh.*

"No loving-kindness for Peter, eh?" I said as I punched the button to retrieve his message.

"Hey, Candi, it's your brother. Mom fell and . . . she's in the hospital. The doctors said if you want to see her . . . before she . . . before she. . . ." My heart stuttered as I heard the emotion in his voice. "Before she . . . uh . . . dies, you need to get here within the next twenty-four hours."

⌇

After the loving-kindness experience, my now-open heart made the final week of Mom's life excruciating to bear witness to. The morning after Peter's call, my sister and I flew into Chicago Midway—me from San Francisco after a harrowing middle-of-the-night ride across the California mountains and hours in the sky, Maggie from Fort Lauderdale. When we landed, we learned that while we were in the air, Peter, by virtue of medical power of attorney, had authorized a Hail Mary surgery on Mom. "Tell the surgeon to wait until we get there," I ordered as Maggie and I navigated the car-rental queue at Midway. "We'll be there in ninety minutes."

I tucked the phone against my shoulder, scribbled a signature on the contract, and mouthed a thank-you to the accommodating Alamo agent.

"He won't wait," Peter said. "He says it will take you longer than that with rush-hour traffic." I motioned to Maggie to put our luggage in the trunk.

"Put him on." I shoved the paper with directions to the toll road at my sister, then cranked the ignition. She body directed me as I fought on the phone with the surgeon.

"No. We can't wait. Time is of the essence," the surgeon said.

"What are the odds she'll make it out of the surgery alive?"

"Not good. Maybe 10 percent."

"Then wait! You have to wait! Please . . . wait!"

"Sorry, ma'am . . . your brother is in charge, and he's already given the approval."

"You tell him to wait," I screamed when the surgeon handed back the phone to Peter.

"They've already prepped her," Peter said. "Mom told me to do whatever it takes to keep her alive." I heard his voice catch. "The surgeon says it's now or never."

I slalomed through traffic and ran a red light. "Hold the phone up to her ear," I directed, then put my phone on speaker. "Mom? We are on the way. We love you," Maggie and I echoed.

Peter came back on the line. "Did she understand? Does she understand we are on the way?" I pressed.

"She nodded her head," Peter said, barely intelligible from the emotion in his voice.

"Tell her to hang on until we get there."

∼

I wish I could report a chick-flick miracle ending where my mother waxed poetic about her feelings for me. And that she and I exchanged heartfelt declarations of love. That we'd asked and received forgiveness for our respective trespasses before she gently transitioned.

Instead, she never regained consciousness after the surgeon butchered her and then forced her to undergo days of water torture. Her kidneys had failed, but he ordered bags and bags of IV fluids and a pharmaceutical kidney shock treatment to flood her system. Her eighty-two-year-old organs were past the point of a jump start, so the fluids built up in her frail body. She'd entered the hospital weighing eighty-five pounds, and died a week later weighing over 150 pounds from the chemically induced hydration.

As the week wore on, the fluid buildup weakened her fragile dermis like a swollen lake breaching a dam. Fluid leaked from old injection sites, first in trickles, then in little geysers. Nurses mummified her limbs with yards of gauze, avoiding medical tape for fear of pulling off sheets of skin during dressing changes.

I pressed the hospital pharmacist, Eric, to keep her doped up. There was a marble-sized knot between her brows I suspected was from severe pain. I clutched at his hand and pleaded, "See that knot? Make it go away. Please make her comfortable." *Comfortable. As in, amp up that morphine. Do you hear me, Eric? Are you picking up what I am laying down? Please don't make me watch this. Please don't let her suffer. For the love of God, Eric, put us out of her misery.*

If Mom had gone into the hospital days . . . even hours before the loving-kindness wave had washed over me, I would have thought, *Ding-dong, the witch is dead*, and asked when the proceeds from her estate would be disbursed. But post-loving-kindness was open-heart surgery for me without anesthesia—deep cuts, nerves raw and abraded, wounds oozing guilt and shame. If I had been a better daughter, she would have been a better mother. She was mentally ill—why hadn't I sought help for her? Why hadn't I acquiesced to her request to accompany me on my Minnie Winnie adventure? Maybe it wouldn't have taken a dramatic loving-kindness experience to get my attention. "I'm sorry we didn't get it right in this lifetime, Mom. I'm so sorry. I'm so so so sorry," I said, stroking her forehead, hoping to dial down that knot of pain.

Maggie and I set up camp at the hospital. We kept the lights dim and played the one album of soothing music on my iPod on a constant loop. To this day, I can't listen to tracks from Deuter's *Earth Blue* without experiencing vivid, painful flashbacks. We shared photos of Mom with the hospital staff—*This is our mother; please see*

*her as the vibrant being she was and not merely the bloated comatose*
*woman in Room 736.*

Our then-octogenarian Aunt Dolores—Mom's last surviving sib-
ling—took a bus from Madison, Wisconsin, to Chicago, then another
bus to South Bend, to sit by Mom's side and pray her back to health.
Aunt Dolores had her own playlist—a constant loop of Hail Marys
frequently punctuated by "Yahweh!" and "in His name."

The day after Mom's surgery, Peter's future son-in-law, Josh,
suffered a mortal brain injury in a snowmobile accident and was on
life support. Peter's attention was splintered between two terminal
situations—Josh's doctors holding out no hope for life, and Mom's
surgeon tantalizing Peter and Aunt Dolores with the false hope Mom
would recover. Peter would stop in for a few minutes, tell our dis-
tended and unconscious mother she was looking good and would
rally soon according to the surgeon. Maggie and I seethed with anger
and frustration over Peter's denial of her situation. After his brief
visits, Peter, Maggie, and I would adjourn to the hall to avoid upset-
ting Aunt Dolores, then whisper a furious defense for our respective
positions on when to pull the plug—Maggie and I on the "open your
eyes, Peter" side, and Peter on the "I promised her I would do whatever it took to keep her alive" side.

Two days post-surgery, Maggie and I returned to the hospital
from the nearby budget hotel where we'd showered and catnapped.
An unfamiliar medical contraption crowded the corner where
Aunt Dolores sat vigil. She didn't know what it was for, she said,
only that it was delivered per the surgeon's orders. Maggie and I
trooped out to the nurses' station and asked for an explanation.
Angie, the nurse who dotted the *i* in her name with a smiley face
when she signed in on the marker board in Mom's room at the
beginning of her shift, beckoned us into a consultation room, then

closed the door. "We didn't want to start without the two of you here," she said.

"Start what?" I asked.

"It's a feeding tube."

"Oh that motherf—" I started.

"Yep, that's why we wanted to wait. Once that goes in. . . ." She trailed off. I knew what it meant: years on life support and court battles to terminate.

"What do we need to do to stop it from going in?" I asked.

"Well . . . your brother has medical power of attorney, so there's nothing the two of you can do except try to convince him it's not in her best interest," Angie said, then shifted from foot to foot. "There's something you should know. Surgeons need to keep their patients alive for three days so that it doesn't count against them."

I shook my head. "Count against them?"

Angie lifted her hands palms up. "It's a numbers game. If a patient dies within three days of surgery, it's reported as a surgical failure; after three days, the 'blame,'" she said, making air quotes, "falls on the hospital."

"So, he doesn't care about her, just about how it looks for him," I said in disgust.

"That guy? Yeah."

"If it was your mom?" I asked.

Angie was definitive. "No way would I let it happen. The surgeon will let up once his time passes."

That afternoon, we learned Mom had contracted MRSA, a virulent staph infection. "You can't touch her without protection," the nurses said, showing us the cart with blue plastic gowns, stiff, scratchy face masks, and boxes of gloves. She was always untouchable, I wanted to tell them.

We'd staved off the feeding tube by running out the surgeon's clock. True to Angie's prediction, we didn't see him once Mom passed into hospital-blame territory. Maggie and I talked with Mom's long-time physician, Dr. London, now that primary care had transferred to her. Dr. London was straightforward: Mom had almost zero chance of returning to consciousness, and if by some miracle she did, would have virtually no quality of life. We asked her to call Peter and let him know the dismal prognosis.

Maggie and I called him after Dr. London did; he was at Josh's funeral. Peter still wasn't willing to go back on his promise to Mom; "almost zero chance" meant there was still a chance. We said we respected his position and role as medical power of attorney, but we could no longer bear to witness Mom's torture from the extreme medical measures.

When he heard we were planning to leave the following morning, Peter relented and agreed to pulling the plug. I ran down the hallway to the nurse's station, thrust my cell phone toward the charge nurse, and sobbed, "He's saying it's time!" I don't think Peter could have handled agreeing in person to terminate Mom's care—he needed distance from the decision . . . needed us to be the bad guys who insisted he renege on his promise to keep Mom alive no matter what.

Maggie and I garbed up and went into Mom's room. Aunt Dolores was stationed in her corner, which was now devoid of the feeding-tube equipment. Her eyes were closed. "Aunt Dolores?" She shifted in the chair, stretched her neck, then opened her eyes. "Aunt Dolores . . . it's . . . time."

I saw confusion settle on her face. "Time?" she asked, her voice thin and reedy.

"It's time . . . to . . . let Mom . . . go," I said, my own voice thin and reedy with emotion.

"But . . . the surgeon said . . . and Peter said. . . ." Her eyes flooded with tears. "I don't understand . . . they said she was getting better."

I sat in the chair next to her, my plastic gown hissing and muttering as I turned to meet her teary gaze. I took her gloved hand in mine. "She's not getter better. She's not ever going to get any better."

"Ohhhhhh." A solitary syllable. Plaintive. Painful. Piteous.

Maggie and I hiccup-sobbed a description of the next steps: A Catholic chaplain was on the way to administer final rites. Tubes would be pulled. Assistive machines stilled. Dr. London said to say final goodbyes because Mom would go in under ten minutes once life support was terminated.

We wept and bid farewell to Mom as Aunt Delores increased the volume and fervor of her prayers. I clawed the mask from my face and ripped off my gloves and gown. Maggie gasped at the breach of protective protocol. I'da gladly taken a megadose of antibiotic and a hazardous-material-decontamination shower for the opportunity of skin-to-skin contact Mom and I so very seldom had.

Aunt Dolores held Mom's left hand, I held Mom's right hand, and Maggie held my hand as we each urged Mom in our own way to let go of life. It felt tribal and ritualistic . . . profound . . . to be a part of a maternal lineage—sister and daughters—companioning Mom as she left the earthly plane. She took her own time, though, doing it her way until the very end. Instead of the predicted ten minutes, Mom held on for four hours, dying fifty years almost to the exact minute of the date and time her own mother died.

# Chapter 10

Now, six years after Mom's death, sitting in my Toyota in the parking lot of the Inn at Saint Mary's after a memorably unmemorable breakfast, I watched as cars splashed through puddles left behind after the previous evening's storm, rooster tails of water arcing and baptizing the shoulders of Dixie Highway. Downed tree limbs, victims of the wicked wind of the west, littered the Saint Mary's campus, the branches beseeching their former perches. "Take me back," I imaged each one pleading to their oak or maple home base, "I belong to you. I am a part of you. This ragged, jagged break fits right *there.*

I checked my phone. Still no call from my birth mother. I tested it the way you do when a hoped-for call from that guy doesn't come; I called myself—the phone went to voice mail. Texted myself; got it immediately. *Well shit, the phone works . . . which means Mary is intentionally not calling me back.*

I leaned my head back against the headrest and sighed, feeling safe and cocooned in the car. I reclined the driver's seat. *Guide me, Mom,* I implored my years-dead mother. *You got me here; now what am I supposed to do?* Departing inn guests thunked closed the doors of a neighboring SUV, bringing my attention back to full consciousness. I ratcheted the seat back to full mast, then chugged half a bottle of water.

*It's 9:00 a.m. Quit stalling. Do something or go home.*

"Screw it. I'm calling Maureen." I rummaged through my messenger bag and pulled out the BeenVerified file. I smoothed the top paper in the folder—the profile on Mary's oldest sister, Maureen Vogel. I had a profile on each of Mary's sisters, and her twin daughters, based on the names I'd found in my birth brother's obituary. I'd pulled a profile on myself and on my daughter to gauge the quality of the database's information. The service had gotten some minor details wrong about our information, but overall I was 90 percent confident I had current and accurate information on where the womenfolk of my birth people lived, and with whom.

I knew of course where Maureen and her husband, Warren, lived—I'd gawked and gaped at Warren the previous afternoon during my ineffectual stalking of Mary's house. According to Loretta from Catholic Charities, Mary hadn't mentioned her pregnancy to any of her siblings. Maureen is Mary's "Irish twin," with barely a year difference in age between them. With nine kids in the family, I was betting the two oldest girls shared a room . . . and, hopefully, secrets.

I turned the phone over and over in my right hand. *What are you going to say to her?* "Howdy . . . we kin!" *Or maybe,* "I think your sister dropped something fifty-eight years ago." I bunched my cropped hair into a tight knot with my left hand and tugged hard. *Uuuuck . . . I don't knoooooow!* I tucked my hands between my knees and took a deep breath. "Alrighty, kiddo, getcho' shit together." I lifted the phone and held it to my chest. "Please, God, don't let me fuck this up."

I rechecked the printout, then pressed in her phone number.

One ring. I huffed out a Lamaze transitional-labor breath.

Second ring.

*I'm gonna hang up. Gonna say,* "Sorry, wrong number!"

Third ring.

*No one home, thankyouJesus . . . voice mail in three, two—*

"Hello?" Male voice.

Internal cartoon gulp. "Hello," I said in my best Time Life operator voice, "Is Mrs. Vogel available?"

There was a hesitation on his end. *Uh-oh, had Mary warned him I was on the loose?*

"Sure, just a moment," he said. *Why did I throw out that Dunkin' Donuts bag? I need to breathe into it.*

"Hello?" Sweet. Pleasant. Slightly quizzical. No obvious signs of concern.

"Hi, my name is Candi Byrne." No gasps of alarm, so I went on, nose prickling with pre-tears. "I don't know any other way to say this, but I'm pretty sure your sister Mary . . . is my birth mother."

I gnawed on my knuckles to stay quiet and let the news land.

"Well, hello, dear," she said after a moment, "We always thought you'd be a boy."

∽

Maureen immediately agreed to meet me at her house after a noontime appointment. "My children are adopted," she said, "so I have a sense of what you're going through. My daughter has reunited with her natural family, but my son has no interest. Maybe I should have him come by to meet you."

"Owww . . . not a good idea; Mary said no one in the family knows about me."

Maureen demurred, then said how much she was looking forward to meeting me. "I'll call you as soon as I'm back from my appointment." I thanked her for her immediate and positive response to my request to meet. *Unlike your sister,* I was tempted to add.

I let the phone fall from my sweaty hand to the floor. Whew! Another hard thing done. D.O.N.E. Done. I fingered away the beads of perspiration on my upper lip. Sipped water. *Mary has an adopted niece and nephew? Interesting. Surely Maureen and Mary have talked about Maureen's experience with adoption. How had Mary kept from revealing what she'd gone through? Had it given Mary a sense of comfort to think about someone like Maureen mothering the baby Mary had given away? If she only knew I went to a Delphine, not a Maureen.*

With hours until Maureen was available, I pondered how to fill the time. I glanced across the street, then smiled and *hmmm*ed as I started the car. Minutes later, I pulled into a parking space in front of the Our Lady of Fatima retreat center on the edge of the Notre Dame campus. I remembered my mother ushering second-grader me down a hallway in the sprawling brick building to the gift shop. I'd been drawn to a tall wooden display rack brimming with rows of holy cards featuring the Blessed Virgin. The cards, about the size of the Salem cigarette pack that was never more than arm's length from my mother, were rendered in dreamy blues, with pops of red and pink. My favorites were the cards embellished with a gold halo or wreath of gold stars around Our Lady's head. I'd coveted those cards. I don't recall if I asked for one or knew that if I asked, my want would be denied. We were there on a mission—to buy a first-communion kit for me: a child-sized white rosary and miniature missal with gilded-edged pages tucked into a clear pouch with a white metal snap.

Mom made an impulse purchase for herself—a "Pray the Rosary" booklet. I found it while sorting through her belongings after she'd died. The edges of its blue covers were creased and curled, the binding repaired multiple times with age-yellowed Scotch tape. She'd stapled to the back cover a card with prayers typed on our IBM Selectric. The inside of the front cover held a card with a rosary-praying cheat sheet written in her hand. The date indicated she'd turned to heavy-duty bead-fingering in 1981 after Dad exited their thirty-year relationship for a woman just five years older than I was.

I got out of the car, wondering what it said about Mom and me that she'd treasured the rosary booklet but hadn't kept my first-communion keepsakes. I ambled over the meticulously manicured grass to the Lady of Fatima tableau sheltered by soaring evergreens. A white stone statue of Our Lady towered fifteen feet. From her perch, she gazed upon three white-stone children kneeling in adoration. Two stone lambs brought up the rear. The Blessed Virgin was in sharp relief against the blue sky. I moved around until her head blocked the sun, creating a semblance of the golden aura on the holy cards.

Popcorn brain. *Mom. Mary. And Mary, the Blessed Virgin. Why am I here? Why didn't anyone come with me? Why didn't I make anyone come with me? Hail Mary full of grace . . . I think there's a picture of me in my communion outfit standing here. Mom and Mary. This Mary, not birth-mom Mary. Am I ruining an old lady's life? Am I ruining mine? Hail Mary . . . I'm alone. No, I know I'm really not . . . but . . . kinda am. Hail Mary . . . Hell, Mary, what am I doing here? Nope, this is* not *helping. What am I going to do for the next*—I pulled my phone from my bra and checked the time—*four hours until I meet with Maureen?*

An idea filtered through my frenetic thoughts: I needed a big dose of my brother-in-law Terry and sister-in-law Bunny. Needed to be in the company and comfort of family. Needed to hear Terry's auctioneer-paced chatter and Bunny's quick wit. I may have divorced Brendan, but I'd retained shared custody of Terry and Bunny.

No matter that I hadn't seen them since my mother's funeral years ago; Terry gave me a warm welcome when I called asking to hang out until an "appointment" I had. "Of course," he said. "Bunny's in town though and won't be back for a while."

I squinted at the dashboard clock and calculated if I could make it to their home and back—forty minutes each way—before my afternoon rendezvous with Maureen. "Well . . . I want to tell you guys together about my, um, appointment; can I come by tonight?"

"Sure, but why don't you meet up with Bun now, since she's in town?" Totally typical Terry that he didn't press about my "appointment"; if I'd planned to reveal a cancer diagnosis or sexual-reassignment surgery, he'd wait till I was ready to talk. He gave me directions to the diner where Bunny was having breakfast with one of their grandsons and said he'd text her a heads-up I was coming.

~

I walked into the mom-and-pop diner, the interior dark and shadowy. The bright May sunshine wasn't powerful enough to melt the years of dusty grease from the small round windows along the top of the outer wall. The smell of bacon, pancakes, and industrial coffee settled into my pores; I knew I'd carry the scent of it in my clothes and hair for hours.

I spotted Bunny and a good-looking young man at a four-top in the middle of the diner. Tears threatened as I walked toward the kind and comforting woman I'd known for over forty years. Aside from the threads of age in her curly blonde crop, she looked the same as when I'd met her so long ago—smooth, pale, freckled skin; elfin tip-tilted nose; and a ready smile.

Terry had filled her in—I was on a secret mission I'd tell them about when it was over. And just like Terry, she respected the request to debrief them later. We chatted about life, love, and the Universe as her shy grandson worked his way through a stack of French toast and a heap of bacon. He showed neither ire at nor interest in my sudden and disruptive company.

After he finished eating, Bunny suggested we wait out the time until Maureen's call at my niece Kathy's house. Kathy and her family live in the house where Terry and Bunny had lived for decades. It had been a second home for me from the time I was a teenager dating Brendan and was where we'd land when traveling to South Bend during our married and parenting years.

Warmth bloomed in my heart as I parked in front of the Tudor-style home in a neighborhood near Notre Dame. I flashed on all the times I'd sat in Bunny's kitchen, tucked into the little breakfast nook as she bustled around either preparing a feast or cleaning up after a meal. So many good conversations—easy, light, familial.

Kathy greeted me warmly, as if I'd seen her yesterday and not a dog's year ago. Bunny, Kathy, and I went into the sunroom, a cozy spot with curl-up-in furniture, fireplace, and natural light coming through the tall, wall-to-wall windows on three sides. I sat with my phone on my lap waiting for the call from Maureen. Kathy was very curious about my sudden appearance in South Bend, so I sketched out the circumstances and promised to give the full story after I'd met with Maureen. Bunny was adamant I stay with her and Terry afterward; Kathy said she and her family would be there too, so I would be supported or celebrated depending on the outcome of the visit.

My phone vibrated. "It's Maureen," I whispered. Bunny and Kathy grabbed hands and began chanting in a low hum—a well-oiled prayer machine. Just before pushing the button to connect with Maureen, I smiled, recalling one of Bunny's boys saying Bunny and Kathy were prayer slingers, whipping out rosaries from a holster, fast on the prayer draw. I felt their love and energy envelop me, and I was glad for their holy target practice.

After finalizing plans with Maureen, I disconnected from the call then stood, my heart thudding. "She's ready?" Bunny asked. I nodded, eyes wide. "Do you want us to go with you?"

I fiddled with the phone. "I think I have to do this part alone," I said, "But I will definitely take you up on staying with you tonight."

"Good. Come right afterward and tell us everything."

Kathy said, "I know you have your own talismans, but I want you to have this," offering a circlet of pea-sized brown wooden beads spaced along a cord, anchored by a chunky wooden cross. She explained it was a rosary she'd gotten in Rome during the installation of Francis as pope. "It was blessed by him," she added.

Tears welled in my eyes. "You can keep the rosary, but I'll want this back," she said, presenting me with a small silver Celtic cross, also blessed by the pope. I dropped my head, tears spilling onto my blouse. *Oh, how I love these people who love me. They're sending me out prayed up. My own sister refused to go with me, but these two are ready to ride shotgun.* I pressed my hand across my mouth and looked up, their faces like a watercolor from the distortion of my tears. I blinked the two of them back into focus and worked my lips between my teeth. I couldn't speak, so I just nodded like a bobblehead doll as I walked to the front door.

I got in the car, tucked the Celtic cross in my bra near my heart, and pulled away, weeping from their love bomb. I fumbled in my purse for tissues and thought, *They are my family. These people who'd known me as Brendan's sixteen-year-old switcheroo girlfriend*—he'd dropped Sandy for Candi in the space of an evening. His family had shrugged, then hugged me, and I'd been in their orbit ever since. Byrnes take in strays—dogs, cats, people—and you're in for life. No judgment. No expectations. No obligations. Just "Hello, you're here, we love you." Haven't seen each other in five years? Doesn't even warrant a mention. "Ya hungry? Tired? Need a kidney?"

I learned how to do family from the Byrnes. I married Brendan to officially be a Byrne. How is it that I could feel a belongingness with them that I never felt as part of my adoptive family? I wasn't blood kin with the Byrnes and yet I felt more integrated with them than with the people who'd bought and paid for me. The Byrne clan talked to me, listened to me, cheered me on, and, from the start, had extended their familial embrace to include my sister. They love my babies and grandbabies. We've got history. We've put in the time. We've endured, no matter how sporadic our connections.

~

I drove down Buchanan's Poplar Street in the opposite direction from the day before. Based on Maureen's directions, I realized I'd gotten it wrong about where they lived: Mr. Dickies Pants I'd seen yesterday was not my uncle after all.

The Saint Joe River glimmered on my left, popping in and out of view from between the houses. Every manicured yard had a boat, or toy-hauler trailer, evidence of the serious-work-and-serious-play ethic in these parts. It was a good bet that most of the male residents worked for or were retired from some sort of tradesman or blue-collar union job—factory, municipal work, or tool-and-die shop. They fished and hunted and tinkered with engines. Meat-and-potatoes guys.

I checked the numbers on the mailboxes and slowed as they counted down to Maureen's address. My heart rate quickened as I approached a long, low brick rambler sprawled across a large wedge of the cul-de-sac where Poplar Street ended. Some manner of watercraft or outdoor-recreation machine was carefully and lovingly draped to the left of the house. I could see a kneeling figure tending a plot of flowering shrubs in the front yard.

*Oh God. Oh Shit. This is really it.* My mouth was dry. *I could bolt . . . put the pedal to the metal and do a* Dukes of Hazzard *donut and rocket back the way I came.*

Tempting.

Cowardly.

"Right, cuz ya know," I said, flicking on my left blinker, "you gotta get this shit *done*."

The figure rose as I turned into the driveway and resolved into a compact man, late seventies, balding, skin weathered into walnut hide. He dusted his hands on the legs of his faded work pants as I got out of the car, then stepped toward me. My breath came fast and shallow and shaky. My prolific chattering mind monkeys went unnaturally silent . . . not even a single utterance as he drew close.

He stopped an arm's length away, and I watched a smile brighten his face and his eyes fill with tears. "Honey," he said, his voice breaking, "we've been thinking about you since the day you were born."

My eyes flooded as relief and joy surged through my body. I hiccupped a sob, then stepped into his open arms for a hug. His wiry arms wrapped around me, his embrace strong and welcoming and more paternal than any I'd ever experienced from my dad. His shirt smelled sunbaked and breeze-filled, and I knew without looking that there was a clothesline in the yard. We stayed huddled, and I inhaled top notes of his clean sweat and the loamy earth he'd been digging in.

He released me then produced a handkerchief from his pants pocket, unabashedly swiping at his eyes. I snuffed and grinned, then pulled a tissue from my pocket. "We're leaky," I said. He nodded and chuckled, then tucked away the hanky.

"Maureen's waiting for you," he said, gesturing toward the front door.

"I've got something for her," I said, pointing the key fob at my car to pop the trunk. I lifted out a hanging basket of pink and purple petunias I'd picked up at a garden center in Buchanan and handed it to him. "Oh, you didn't need to bring flowers," he said. "Heh-heh . . . she's got me as her blooming idiot!"

I loved him on the spot.

"I have another one, for . . . um . . . Mary," I said, pulling out a basket of purple and white petunias. "I don't know if I'll . . . get to see her, so would you . . . give it to her? From me. Please?"

"I'll put it right here in the shade, and we'll make sure she gets it," he said, toting both baskets toward the house. I heard him say something else as I opened the back door to grab the tablet I'd loaded with pictures of my family. "Sorry, what did—"

My breath caught. A tall, lean woman stood on the wide brick front porch, the sun highlighting a halo of short white hair. She looked like an L.L. Bean model for their angel collection, dressed casually and simply—khaki slacks and a tailored wash-and-wear cotton-blend blouse. A beatific smile and sparkling eyes glowed in her naturally smooth-skinned face.

Her welcoming gaze was like a tractor beam, pulling me home toward the mothership. Dazed, I walked toward her, my heart stuttering and pounding against my ribcage. For the first time in my fifty-eight years of life, I was in the company of a member of my birth tribe. *We share DNA. We are blood. I am one of you.*

I stepped onto the porch, and we embraced wordlessly and easily. My heart slowed and steadied in moments, guided by her measured breathing. I sighed in contentment, and she released me to look at my face. I don't know what she saw, but in her, I saw kindness, sweetness, and love. I felt her acknowledge and accept me . . . and extend a long-overdue welcome home.

"Come inside, won't you," she said. "I've got some pictures I'm sure you'll want to see."

I followed Maureen through the foyer and into the front room.

*This feels so . . . natural. Comfortable. Weird, because we are complete and total strangers to each other. Except . . . I guess we're not.* I glanced around the room. It was spotless and company-ready, as I was sure was the rest of the house. The space was large enough to easily accommodate seating for a dozen or more, yet it maintained a cozy feeling. A huge picture window on the front wall offered a view of Warren's landscaping efforts. A well-loved spinet piano hugged the wall between the front room and the kitchen; I imagined there'd been many a family sing-along after dinner. A cream brick fireplace anchored one wall; family photos filled the wooden mantle that I was sure sported timeworn Christmas stockings every December.

Warren had followed us inside and parked himself on the couch. He maintained a constant stream of commentary I almost immediately recognized would go on whether his patter was acknowledged or not. Maureen gestured toward a large square coffee table topped with a photo album and a short stack of framed pictures. "There are pictures in there of your . . . uh . . . Mary, and some with my parents and all of my siblings. Please, make yourself comfortable and take as long as you want to look at the photos." I sat on a love seat across from the fireplace.

"Can I fix you something to eat or drink?" she asked.

"Nothing to eat, thank you. I'm a bundle of nerves!" I said, patting my chest. "I'd be grateful for a glass of water, though."

I bent to the album as she went to the kitchen and Warren filibustered. "You look *so* much like Sharon!" he enthused, referring to one of Mary's twin daughters. "Doesn't she look just like Sharon?" he asked Maureen once she came back with the water. "Looks just like her! Is there a picture of Sharon in that album? There's got to be a picture of Sharon in there. Or maybe that other album. Maureen, where's that other album? I'm gonna get my camera," he said, and launched up from the couch and crossed the foyer. "I'll show the pictures at the family reunion this weekend. Nobody will believe how much the two of you look alike!" I heard him say from another room.

I lifted my chin toward the foyer and raised my volume. "Warren, Mary told the Catholic Charities social worker that no one else in the family knows about me. The social worker said Mary didn't even tell her husband or kids. I don't have any problem with you taking and sharing pictures, but you would absolutely need to check with Mary first." *Much as having to check with her pisses me off.*

Warren came back into the front room, small silver digital camera in hand. "Sharon is your half sister; no wonder you look so much alike. Say cheese!" I looked at Maureen imploringly as he circled me like a paparazzo. Her face read, *I'll handle it.* Warren came in for a close-up. I raised my eyebrows toward Maureen in an "Are you sure?" questioning look. She smiled knowingly and nodded. I took her at her non-word and went back to perusing the album.

She narrated as I flipped through the pages—her parents; siblings; multigenerational family trip to Ireland; Mary as caretaker of their lone cousin, who had special needs. I asked Maureen for permission to take pictures of the pictures. *I might never have a chance to see Mary in person.* Then I shared the pictures of my kids and granddaughters with her, hoping she would gasp in recognition at any Flynn-family traits. She was complimentary of how good-looking they were, but their noses, eyes, and ears were left unclaimed. Warren carried on a monologue, picking up snippets from Maureen's and my conversation and galloping with them like the Pony Express. I took my cue from Maureen and let his river of words flow over and around me.

After I finished with the photos, Maureen asked me to tell her again how I came to be on Mary's doorstep yesterday. She marveled

at how Aunt Dolores's vision led to a successful search in mere minutes after years of disappointments. "It was divine intervention, for
sure," I said.

"What is your next step, dear? Are you going to try Mary again?"
Maureen asked, leaning in my direction as Warren stitched the air
with his thoughts on divine intervention.

"Well," I said, pausing to tap a knuckle against my lips, "she hasn't
called me back, so I'm pretty sure I . . . scared her," I said, wincing at
the likelihood that my son was right—I'd ruined an old lady's life for
my own selfish purposes. "I'm thinking that anything further would
have to come from . . . you," I said, unfurling my hands toward her.

She straightened in her chair and looked out the picture window.
I continued, "If she heard from you that you'd met me and that I was
a nice person—"

Maureen turned to me. "A *very* nice person," she interrupted
with fervor, then smiled her angelic smile.

"A very nice person," Warren echoed, then switched back to his
riff about how much Sharon and I looked alike.

I put both hands over my heart and nodded thanks. "If she heard
from you that I was a *very nice person*, then she might be open to
meeting me," I finished, then sat back to let her ponder. *Come on. . . .
Do it! Do it! Do it!* The thought was disconcerting; it felt so self-serv-
ing and manipulative. *But it's not*, I argued with myself. *I just want
what's mine.*

Warren prattled as Maureen pondered. "Just like her! It's amazing. It's not just your size either. It's your face. Don't you think it's her
face, Maureen?"

"Okay," Maureen said, "I'll do it."

Maureen went into the kitchen to make the call. I imagined her
picking up the handset of a wall-mounted phone whose curly cord

snaked around itself in a double helix, then taking a deep breath before punching in Mary's phone number. *How do I say this?* I felt her thinking. *How do I break this kind of news?*

Warren was crying, mopping at his face with the same cotton square he'd used when meeting me. I wanted to offer words of consolation, but I'd tuned in late and had no idea about whom he lamented or why. I tilted my head and made a moue of my mouth, nodding occasionally and *hmmm*ing in ersatz sympathy. I strained to hear Maureen in the kitchen on the phone with Mary. "Do you understand who I'm talking about?" was the only thing I clearly heard her say over the noise of Warren's weeping. Moments later, she was back in the front room, not the least bit fazed by her husband's tears.

She sank into her chair and let out a breath. I couldn't tell from her face or that breath if she'd been successful. "Mary said she will come down."

*Woohoo! High five, Maureen!* "But she has two conditions." *Uh-oh.* I braced for them. "First, she said she can only stay fifteen minutes because she's on her way up north for her granddaughter's piano recital."

My gut twisted in a flash of anger: *Hey, no fair . . . she's got two grandkids who were first in line.*

"Okaaaay."

"And the second . . . is that no one in the family outside of the four of us can know about you."

Another blast of anger, but longer and hotter. *Still with this secret thing? It is 2014!* I could feel prickles of sweat carpet my scalp and upper lip. *There is no goddamn stigma against adoption anymore. Has she not watched* Oprah? *What the fucking fuck?* I sipped at the glass of tepid water, hoping it would help quell my ire. Maureen waited patiently as I processed the second condition.

"Okay," I said a minute later, "I'll agree to that." *For the moment. Until I get what I want. Until I don't get what I want.*

"Good . . . because she's on her way."

*Ho-ly shit . . . it worked!*

"She said she thought the door had been closed on this," Maureen said, settling back in her chair.

I leaned forward and traced the edge of the coffee table with my fingers. "Well, I did tell Catholic Charities to tell her no one from their agency would ever call her again." Had I unconsciously thought to language that statement so specifically to leave open a loophole . . . an "Aunt Delores has a vision" loophole?

Warren looped back yet again to the Sharon-and-Candi show: "Wait'll she sees you! You and Sharon could be sisters . . . er, are sisters. Half sisters." More photos. Click. Click. Click. "And wait till everyone sees these pictures!"

"No!" Maureen and I exclaimed at the same time. Warren was startled into blessed silence. Maureen reminded him of Mary's insistence that no one other than the four of us could know about my existence.

"Maybe she'll change her mind," Warren offered, turning the camera in his hands.

"Maybe . . . we'll have to see how things go," Maureen murmured. "Until then, no one else sees the photos, dear." Warren nodded solemnly, then brightened and revved up about his antique car—the tarped treasure I'd seen in the side yard.

Maureen chatted about her parents and grandparents. I tried to stay tuned in, but the knots in my stomach writhed and tightened in a hot pulse. *I'm about to tap into the motherlode after years of emotional drilling. I never wanted to be here in the first place. What do I want from this meeting? What's the endgame?* Echoes of my son's indictment added to the churn—"You're going to ruin an old lady's life so you can have closure?" *It's not my fault, damn it! I wouldn't be here if she had just sent me some damn pictures all those years ago.*

I fiddled with the silver labyrinth pendant my daughter had given me for good luck, my mind circling around the idea of closure. *Closure. If I ask* them *about my birth father, I won't have to press her. Brilliant! And oh so noble.* I sat upright and tapped interlaced fingers against my lips. "Um . . . I want to ask," I said, opening my hands to them, "do you know anything about my birth father?"

Warren maintained his monologue and Maureen's composure didn't waver, but the energy in the room changed. I felt the mental telepathy of long-marrieds spark between them:

*Should we tell her?*

*We don't know for sure if it's him.*

*But it had to be him, right? Let's tell her.*

*Dear, it's not our place to say.*

*Then what do we tell her?*

*I think we should say it is better to come from Mary.*

Warren shifted from his car talk. "A group of us guys from my high school used to hang around with a group of girls from Maureen and Mary's high school. From the minute I laid eyes on Maureen, I had eyes for no other."

I mentally scratched my head about his profession of early love for Maureen. *Oh I get it . . . he's making it clear* he's *not my father!*

"We really don't know for sure who it might be," Maureen demurred. "There was a group of us, as Warren said."

*Hmmm. Interesting. Was Mary seeing more than one guy? Oh god, was it a rape? No . . . Warren would have told me he'd kicked the rapist's ass.*

I nodded slowly. "Okay." Rocked my head side to side. "Okay,"

I repeated, then leaned back. "I just needed to ask." *I'll get it out of Mary. By all that is holy I'll get her to tell me.*

A red pickup truck arrowed into the driveway. "There's Mary," Maureen caroled. *Well, well, well . . . that was her truck I saw last night after all. Like mother like daughter,* I marveled, thinking back on the "Real Women Drive Trucks" bumper sticker pasted to the tail end of the Isuzu pickup I drove for years.

I saw a sturdy woman with sensibly cropped white hair pop out from behind the wheel, a serious "let's get this done" expression on her face.

"She'll come barreling in like a bulldog," Warren said.

She disappeared from view on the far side of the house, away from the front door. "She usually comes in the back door," Warren said.

Maureen rose and walked toward the back door. "We're not going to say anything, dear, okay?" Maureen said over her shoulder to Warren. "We'll just let her come in."

A minute passed. Then another.

*What's taking her so long? Did she change her mind? Is she standing there wondering what to do? She's alone out there and I'm in here with her people.* I stood. Maureen continued, "God love her. Bless her . . . that's what the Irish would say."

"Irish, yeah. I have this Celtic cross my niece, Kathy, gave me," I said, patting my chest where the pope-blessed crucifix rested against my heart. "She insisted I carry it with me today." I took a deep breath as we waited . . . and waited for Mary to come through the door. "God is good," Maureen said. "He loves us all so much. He is giving us this moment."

At the single brisk knock, Warren yelled from the front room, "C'mon in, Mare," as Maureen opened the door. Mary stepped inside and wordlessly embraced her sister. After a moment, Maureen rubbed Mary's back, then gave her a squeeze before disengaging.

Mary turned toward me, and I studied her from across the room. Maybe five feet tall. Flushed round cheeks. Blue eyes glittering behind wire-frame glasses. *That's my nose. And those are my ears.* Mouth and jaw ravaged from mouth cancer. *From holding in her secret.*

*It's her. It's really her.* The woman who'd been almost theoretical—a condition, a circumstance, a mystery—was real. A seventy-something pickup-truck driver with tears threatening to spill down onto the front of her JCPenney peasant blouse. She'd borne four children, raised three, lost two—one to the times in which she'd given birth to me, and one well before his time. She was sister, aunt, mother, grandmother, and survivor—just like me. I took a tentative step forward. She opened her arms wide, and I was across the room in a heartbeat.

We clung to each other in a tight hug for a long moment, my head angled against hers to close the gap between our six inches of height disparity. She pulled her head back slightly, looked up at me, then rose up to kiss me on the mouth. I was surprised by so intimate a gesture. Her lips, puckered and distorted by cancer, presented a facial landscape not difficult or uncomfortable to experience, just different.

She stepped back and took my hands in hers. "Hello," she said, her voice as sweet and lilting as it had been on her answering machine.

"Hello." I swallowed hard. "Thank you for agreeing to see me," I squeaked.

"Sure," she said, and patted my arm. "It was such a shock . . . I was thinking, *Whoa, how did this all come about?*"

I sniffed, then huffed out a laugh. "It was a real surprise to me, too!" I gave her an abbreviated version of how Aunt Delores's vision landed me on her doorstep the day before. "And you weren't home,"

I said, "but I think this worked out better so that you had some time to process the news."

"Well, I heard your voice mail messages yesterday, and I said to myself, 'I don't know any Candi'; I thought you were trying to sell me something." I mentally shook my head. *Ohforgodsake. I was up half the night worrying for nothing.*

"Mary, can you sit and stay for a while?" Maureen asked. Mary nodded; then she and I sat facing each other on the love seat. I gazed at her, then broke into air-gulping sobs. She pulled me close and scrubbed and patted my back. My mind swirled.

*Mother-and-child reunion.*

*I never wanted this!*

*This feels right.*

*This feels wrong!*

*She's a sweet old lady.*

*You're ruining her life!*

*Oh yeah, well she ruined mine first!*

*"Trying to sell her something. . . ."*

I mentally tsked, righted myself, ransomed a tissue from my purse, then blotted my eyes and nose. "I want to assure you, I respect your wishes, and this will stay between us," I said, stirring a circle in the air.

Warren chimed in, "It's just the four of us who know, Mare, now that your mom and dad are gone."

Mary looked at me. "Well . . . not really. I told my husband and kids about you."

I cocked my head. *Whoa. What?* "Loretta—you know, from Catholic Charities—said your family didn't know."

"We all cried so much . . . let's just say it was like Niagara Falls. And then it was over."

*What precipitated* that *conversation? Pregnancy scare with one of her girls? Her son? Did any of them say, "Let's go find her?"* I tucked the questions away for later. I was 99 percent sure she'd agree to a "later." *All in good time, my pretty,* I thought in my best Wicked Witch of the West voice, *all in good time.*

Maureen and Warren excused themselves to give us private time. Mary and I chatted. It was easy to talk with her, perhaps because we both stuck to light stuff . . . work, travel, family. No awkward or uncomfortable silences. No forced conversation. It was not the least bit weird, while, at the same time, totally surreal. And, as I'd thought the day before, so anticlimactic after all the years of angst and effort and drama and Nancy Drew detective work.

I showed her the carefully curated collection of photos I'd loaded onto the tablet, hoping for a spark of recognition—an "ooow, she looks just like my . . . " or "my goodness, he's the spitting image of. . . ." She swiped through the pictures without comment, not lingering on a single photo. *Too painful? Maybe. Too overwhelming? Likely. Not interested? I don't think that's it.* I watched her slide through several shots. *I'm going with overwhelming: "Hello, you've known me for fifteen minutes, now meet the family you could have known all these years."* She handed me the tablet, then launched into a roll call of her family. *Grounding herself in the familiar. I get it, sistah! Uh, mutha.*

She glanced around, then gave a decisive tap on her thighs. "I really wish I had more time. . . ."

*Ohjeez! Gotta get in the biggie before she bolts.* "Uuum . . . are you willing to say anything about my birth father?"

She paused, smoothing the fabric of her perma-press capris. I didn't sense reluctance or hesitation, more that she was rooting through a dusty, long-buried file. After a long moment, she said, "He had dark hair." Seconds ticked by. I waited . . . impatiently rolling a mental hand—*M'kay* . . . aaaand? *Is she picturing him? Does she see him in me?*

"He was very very . . . bossy," she said finally.

We sat in silence, *bossy* echoing in my mind. The idea that it might have been rape came back to me. Much as I wanted to know the paternal part of my equation, I decided not to press her. *For the moment.*

She shifted on the love seat, signaling her imminent departure. I layered my hands against my heart, feeling a point of the pope cross press into the top of my left breast. "Thank you again for agreeing to meet me."

Tears filled her eyes. "I'm really glad I decided to come." She leaned toward me, and I met her halfway, our foreheads touching. "I gave birth to you," she whispered. I nodded, and her head bobbed in concert. "I love you," she murmured.

"I love you too," I said. And in that moment . . . I did.

∿

Warren took a picture of Mary and me with my iPhone. The photo shows us smiling, heads tilted together, supportive arms around each other, the cream brick fireplace in the background. It's the kind of picture you'd display in a fancy frame on the mantle. A family photo, fifty-eight years in the making. One I never expected . . . or even wanted to have taken.

The four of us walked out the front door and stood on the porch, more awkward in farewell than we'd been in greeting. A round-robin of "Well. . . ." and "So good to meet you. . . ." and "Stay in touch." Clumsy hugs. Nodding heads. Keys jangling. Mary broke from the clutch first and stepped off the porch onto the driveway. "Oh! I brought you flowers," I said, a child shyly offering posies. "White and purple. Uh, petunias."

"And I will treasure them," Mary said, opening the driver's door of the red pickup. "Warren, will you take care of them until I get back?" she called to her brother-in-law. Practical. Unapologetic. I liked that she didn't make a big deal of the gift, though she was obviously touched by the gesture. Mary hoisted herself into the truck cab, fired up the engine, and confidently and expertly reversed down the drive. She tapped a goodbye on the horn and waved cheerily as she roared up the street.

I took a deep breath then tried to release it slowly, but I felt shaky. Adrenalized. Amped. Pumped. *Take a victory lap, cuz I done did the thing.* I'd seen the pictures and heard a few stories. *I. Did. It.* I mind-danced—jazz hands and shuffle-ball-changes. "Sorry?" I said, realizing Maureen had asked a question.

"Would you like to have lunch with us?"

My body quaked from the shaken-not-stirred cocktail of emotions. My stomach muscles spasmed. My legs quivered like the floppy-limbed scarecrow from *The Wizard of Oz*. This was a familiar feeling . . . it had happened both times after giving birth.

*I just gave birth to a mother.*

"Oh. Uh, no. Thank you. Thank you! No. My family is waiting to either console me or celebrate," I said, my voice quavering.

Maureen smiled and nodded her understanding.

"Have your family come up here," Warren offered. "We love company. They can come up anytime!"

I twirled my keys like a gunslinger spinning a pistol. "That's sweet . . . I'll let them know." I felt chokey, fidgety, and in need of escape. *It's over. I'm done. Veni, vidi, get the fuck outta here.*

# Chapter 11

Two weeks after the adrenaline-fueled, secret agent assault on my birth mother, I crashed. I'd played years of emotional chess—strategizing about how to get the pictures and stories I'd yearned for, then waiting, waiting, waiting . . . only to learn I'd been thwarted once again. I'd played by the rules, but Mary would scatter the pieces, leaving me feeling frustrated and cheated. Finally, after all those years of disappointment and rejection, I'd called off the game, vowing never to play again. Thanks to Aunt Delores's vision, I'd jumped back into competition for the rights to my birthright, because I wanted to know what I think most other adoptees—hell, what most everyone—wants to know: Who and where do I come from? Who do I look like? Who are my people? What is my history? Genealogy is one of the top hobbies in the United States. Whole industries are based on documenting family moments and arranging family reunions. An entire religion is based on identifying ancestral roots and records.

I wanted what most non-adopted people take for granted, what most non-adopted people can do with curiosity and modest resources—to know my history. It's infuriating to have to defend that desire, to be considered pushy or intrusive or "ruining an old lady's life" all because I wanted to know about me. I'm expected to suck it up and carry on and stay in a tiny secret box.

After years of being respectful of her need for secrecy, I was just so . . . done. Everything was on Mary's terms . . . had always been on her terms—from the decision to give me up at birth to refusing contact because no one in her family knew about me to having me back in her life . . . but only if a damn cone of silence was invoked each time we talked. I didn't even want to talk to her . . . except to get answers. I didn't want a relationship. I was forced into it because now she wanted it her way. Mary gets a Candi treat, and I'm left wearing a plus-size trench coat and novelty nose and mustache disguise.

Nobody is putting this given-up baby in the corner.

"Have you talked to your mother?" friends would ask.

"No," I'd say, "she's dead."

"No, no, no," they'd say, "your *real* mother."

"Still dead."

They meant Mary, of course. And they meant well. I was snarky to them because I was uncomfortable about how I was handling the post-reunion portion of the program, which was that I wasn't handling it at all. Mary had left two voice mails I'd never listened to, let alone responded to. Days without contact piled up into weeks, and then heaped into months that I kept us in limbo. I felt guilty—did she think I wasn't contacting her because I was getting her back for not wanting contact with me? And was that a part of it? I tried on a "Here ya go, honey, try another six years of radio silence and see how it feels," but that didn't feel like the reason.

No . . . it was more that I had what I'd come to get, or most of it. Well . . . enough of it to satisfy my curiosity. Okay . . .satisfied enough of my curiosity that I let the rest go so that I didn't have to stay locked in her secret treasure box. I felt ashamed—not because I hadn't listened to or responded to her messages; I felt ashamed because I hadn't voiced to her my anger, my frustration, my outrage, my NFW. I didn't stand up for myself. I wasn't worth fighting for.

That last one held the most heat for me. For my entire life, I'd carried the message that I wasn't worth fighting for—I believed it on a cellular level . . . and . . . I had proof. My birth families had given me away. My adoptive father didn't protect me and my siblings from our mentally ill mother. The cowardly married men I "dated" couldn't . . . wouldn't . . . leave their soulless shrews. Mary wanted me in her life, but only if I stayed a secret. I was special, just not special enough.

~

On the one-year anniversary of our reunion, I felt the need to offer an explanation to Mary for why I hadn't been in contact with her. I needed to speak my truth. And, covertly and less honorably—I wanted to keep the door open to learning from her who my birth father was.

Dear Mary,

I am so sorry to have splashed down in the middle of your life then disappeared. I wigged out after our meeting. I hadn't prepared myself—I was on the road and on your doorstep within forty-eight hours of my aunt having her vision and telling me to never give up connecting with you. Running to Buchanan was a gut reaction; I hadn't the time to think how it might impact or affect either of us.

For fifty-some years, I'd yearned to know who I looked like, and so often now when I look in the mirror, I see parts of you. It's both magical and disconcerting. It is nearly impossible for me to look at the picture Warren took of us—it reminds me of how you opened to receiving me and how I have let a year go by without maintaining a connection with you.

My worst fear is that you feel I may have stayed silent

and out of touch as a way of "getting back" at you for not agreeing to our connecting when Catholic Charities first reached out to you several years ago. I am SO sorry if I caused you even a second of thought about that.

The real reason is that I was afraid to get close to you and yet still have to be a secret. I respect your need for the knowledge of me to remain a secret. But I recognized soon after our meeting that I couldn't abide "sneaking around," as it were. I felt it would make me feel shameful, or something to be ashamed of.

Until very recently, I'd struggled all my life feeling shame and feeling "less than." This past year, the existential part of me has wrestled with the newly emotionally intelligent me— do I follow my ancestry and connection, or do I stay true to myself? And where I've landed is that it doesn't have to be either or—I want to know you; I want you to know me . . . and it doesn't have to go beyond that unless we both agree.

Maybe this is a moot point. Maybe you're closed to further contact because you feel you can't trust me after my "now you see me, now you don't" move. I wouldn't blame you.

I hope, though, that you might be open to reconnecting. We have several traits in common—active, independent, family-oriented, and creative, for starters. I think we could be good friends.

Whatever your decision, please know that I will always think of you with warmth and love. I cherish the memory of our brief time together.

Candi

# Part Two

*The key to the Heroine's Journey is not her reward for victory, but how and why she fights, struggles, and perseveres to the end.*

—B. J. Priester

# Chapter 12

Memorial Day weekend of 2016, I reflected on how it had been two years since my urgent miracle-guided road trip to Michigan and a year since I'd sent Mary the "if you ever decide I'm not a secret anymore . . ." letter. I'd gleaned enough information from her to sate my curiosity about her side of my story, but I was still itching to learn more about my birth father, other than he had dark hair and was "very bossy." Mary had never responded to the missive, which left me with virtually no hope of learning about my birth father . . . at least from firsthand knowledge.

After my surprise meeting with Mary, Maureen, and Warren, I regularly and obsessively scoured the Web for a Northridge High School Class of 1955 yearbook. Warren had said a group of guys from his high school class hung with a group of girls from Mary and Maureen's high school, so I was convinced I'd flip through the Northridge yearbook pages and know at a glance which young man was my birth father. I had no earthly basis for thinking that; it was not a hunch, it was a wish-upon-a-star, find-a-four-leaf-clover, rub-a-genie-lamp fairy tale. But I had to know. . . had to keep looking for that part of who I was.

"What the hell," I said to my computer screen, "Lemme check eBay . . . for the sixteenth dozen time." I plugged the familiar terms into the eBay search bar. My eyes bugged out when I saw the search results—not one, but *two* Northridge High School yearbooks were up for auction. Class of '54 and Class of '56. Buy It Now price: $48.00 each, plus $5.99 shipping.

*Gonna put your money where your magical thinking is?* I had nothing to go on other than the squishy clue from Warren. How big could his crowd have been that he wasn't sure which one of them my birth father might be? I thought back to my high school days when I'd hung with a group of a dozen or so hippie types; we always knew who was paired off with whom, even outside our small circle. My boyfriend at the time, a senior, was tight with his car-mechanic and shop-class buds—no secrets among that crowd about who was canoodling. And as I thought about it, the entire high school population of four hundred could have likely identified couples with near-perfect accuracy.

Maureen and Warren *had* to know. I bristled about having to play amateur detective . . . and pay for guesses they could answer for free. But contacting them would blow the firm boundary I'd set about not engaging in a relationship with Mary built on continued secrecy. I could probably get the truth from yappy Warren, but it would cost me my integrity and freedom—he'd for sure tell Maureen and Mary . . . and lobby for renewed contact. Oy. A hundred bucks for old yearbooks was a bargain compared to that.

I considered the yearbooks—1954 and 1956; did I need both? If my birth father was Class of 1955 like Warren, the 1956 one would be no help. *If* he was class of 1955. *Hmmm* . . . I snapped my finger in an aha and fished through my purse for my go-to decision aid: an amethyst pendulum.

I'd found the pendulum in my daughter's tried-it-and-moved-on stash of spiritual-seeking accoutrements. Over the years we'd switched perspectives on chakras, crystals, and other woo-woo beliefs and practices. She's now a pragmatic boss lady, and I have my energy healer on speed dial. My son was always a zeros-and-ones guy and refers to my spiritual endeavors as "unicorn-fart sniffing."

"Those kids have no idea why they're rolling their eyes right now," I muttered, as the two-inch-long cylindrical purple crystal dangled freely on a fine brass chain from my hand. Pendulums respond to some kind of personal vibrational energy when you ask a yes-or-no question. For me, the crystal swings in a circle for *yes* and back and forth for *no*. I wouldn't base my life on the answer from a twirling rock, but in the absence of hard facts about my birth father, what the hell did I have to lose but a C-note to an eBay seller?

I held the end of the chain between my right finger and thumb at heart level, with the pendulum hanging near my navel. "Is my birth father represented in one of these yearbooks?" I asked out loud. The pendulum immediately began scribing a large circle—an emphatic *yes*.

I stilled the movement with my left hand for the next question. "Is he in the Class of 1954 yearbook?" Again, an immediate large clockwise twirl . . . *yes*.

I brought the movement to a halt. "Is he in the Class of 1956 yearbook?" The pendulum swung in a straight line from north to south . . . *no*.

I nodded, then palmed the amethyst. I hesitated a moment, then let it unfurl and asked, "Is my birth father still alive?" A twitch, then north to south . . . *no*. Sigh. *Another unavailable man . . . the story of my life.* Sadness washed over me—*I will never know him; he will never have known of me*—followed by a sneaker wave of anger—*goddamn secrets!* The tide of hot emotion ebbed as quickly as it had hit, leaving wry bemusement in its wake. *Uuum, helllooo . . . you're getting all worked up over the prognostications of a rock?* I shook my head, shrugged, then completed the purchase of the Northridge High School Class of 1954 yearbook.

∾

The following week, two colleagues, independent of each other, told me about their experiences with a DNA-testing service. For $100, AncestryDNA, an arm of the wildly popular genealogical-search website Ancestry.com, would analyze a small vial of saliva and, within six weeks, return an ethnicity profile. They'd both received surprising results—my Black colleague was shocked to find she had Scandinavian roots. My Puerto Rican colleague couldn't believe she carried a Russian bloodline.

Maybe my results would show I'm Native American or Japanese . . . which would make picking my birth father out of the yearbook infinitely easier. One week later, I eagerly tore open the DNA-test-kit box. Waiting the recommended hour after eating, I spent another hour working up enough saliva to fill the two-inch tube. Lid on, shaky-shaky to activate the preservative, then into the padded envelope went a little piece of myself . . . and a lot of hope.

∾

The yearbook arrived two weeks after the DNA test went to the lab. A musty smell breached the shroud of bubble wrap and kraft paper. The book was much thinner than I expected—barely sixty pages sandwiched between embossed navy-blue covers.

I flipped to the juniors—the Class of 1955. Disappointment. Only the seniors had individual close-ups. The other three grades featured full-body group shots, thirty or more kids each, heads the size of a dime. It shouldn't have surprised me that all the pictures were in black and white . . . more gray tone, actually, with soft contrast. The resolution was terrible. I pulled out a magnifying glass and eyeballed one of the junior class photos. At that magnification, the picture was a study in pointillism, the image a series of dots. I took a test shot with my phone to gauge the level of detail visible when enlarged. All that did was show me bigger dots. My bespectacled eyes would have to do.

There were six group shots in the junior class, two photos to a page. I studied all the males in each photo, no matter the hair color— light gray tone or darker gray tone. I peered at the pages under a strong light, auditioning focal lengths with my arm to get the sharpest focus. No one stood out as I'd hoped would happen. There were a number of dark-haired males, though none that looked particularly bossy.

Pendulum time.

"Is my birth father represented in this yearbook?"

*Yes!*

I had a sudden chilling thought. Even though the pendulum had previously indicated my birth father was dead, I asked, "Is it Warren?"

The pendulum practically leapt north and south—*no!*

Okay, okay. "Is my birth father on this page?"

No to the first page. No to the second page. Yes to the third.

"Is he in this picture?"

*Yes!* My skin prickled and I inhaled sharply.

I held the crystal over the second photo on the page. "What about this picture?"

*No.*

I went back to the "yes" group shot. "Is my birth father in this photo?" I asked again.

*Yes!*

I laid the pendulum down, closed the yearbook, and spent the next hour in avoidance overdrive—doing laundry, scrubbing the kitchen sink, shaking the throw rugs, and losing myself in Pinterest. "What am I avoiding?" I asked myself after tiring of pinning recipes to my "Recipes I'll Probably Never Make" Pinterest board. The answer came right away: If I took the pendulum guidance as truth, (1) I would need to confirm with Mary, Maureen, or Warren whomever the pendulum pointed to was in fact my birth father, and (2) I was pre-exhausted by the notion of having to explain how I'd come to the conclusion it was him. I wasn't ashamed or embarrassed that I used a pendulum, but the confusion or judgment from others? Ugh.

I parked myself at the dining room table where the dark-blue yearbook and purple pendulum sat like an odd still life. Back to the "yes" photo.

Row one?

*No.*

Row two?

*No.*

Row three?

*Yes.*

I started from the left. Him?

*Yes!* to the dark-haired boy on the end of the row. I squinted at the photo. He was cute. Not at all bossy looking. His cheeks would have been fair game for the cupped palms of his grandmother. Under closer scrutiny, I realized he looked much like my ex-husband had when I first met him in his late teens. Had it been a recognition or longing for deep tribal connection that drew me to my ex? Was I a daddy's girl?

*Hey . . . slow down! You don't even know if this is the guy.*

I checked his name—William J. Simpson Jr. *Simpson—what ethnicity is that?* Google to the rescue. British. Not Irish. Not sure I wanted to know I wasn't 100 percent Irish. The one bit of identity I had clung to from my earliest years was "the map of Ireland" on my face, as my mother often said. I was Irish, married a Byrne, named my kids Kelly Michael and Caitlin Colleen. I'd spent two weeks on pilgrimage in Ireland to celebrate my sixtieth birthday. I just couldn't *not* be Irish.

"Could it be anyone else?" I pleaded with the pendulum.

*No.*

~

"Don't you think he looks like us?" I asked my kids during one of our regular family dinners. Caity looked to where I pointed in the yearbook. "Kinda, yeah. But maybe I'm just looking for it."

"What do you think, honey?" I said, turning the book toward my son.

He glanced at the page. "Yeah, I guess. Kinda," he said, then dipped a chip into my famous queso. He crunched and gave a thumbs up to the cheese dip. "How'd you find out it was him?"

"Weeell. . . ."

My pragmatic boy chuffed a laugh. "Oh, let me guess . . . you used the pendulum," he said, putting a mocking, singsongy spin on the last word and rolling his eyes as I knew he would.

I took a chip. Dip. Crunch. "Mmmm . . . it is a good batch, right?" Wiped my mouth. "Hey, you don't have to believe it. All I know is that a yearbook—*two* yearbooks, in fact—became available after months of searching in vain, and I was guided to this one." I stood up and looked my son in his smirky eyes, and double-tapped on the year-book page. "And then I was guided to him." So there.

~

The next day I went back to the Goog to snoop for William J. Simpson Jr. Eighty gabillion results. Narrowed it down with "Northridge High School" and up popped "Class list, Northridge High School Class of 1955." How had this site not popped up before? I clicked and scanned down an alphabetical contact list a dedicated class historian had compiled and saw "William J. Simpson Jr. (Jack), deceased."

I *hmmm*ed and spiraled a lock of hair around my finger. Deceased. The pendulum was right! The class list was one page of an entire site devoted to the NHS Class of 1955. I clicked on "Good Friends Gone" and scrolled down the page, reading memorials and looking at later-in-life photos of men and women who'd died in the six decades since receiving their diplomas.

At the bottom of the page, in a matrix of senior-yearbook pictures, I saw a matured version of the William J. Simpson Jr. I'd seen in the Class of 1954 yearbook. Same dark hair, but shorter, a man's cut. His features were more defined—chin and brow ridge sharper. He looked serious . . . brooding, even. Bossy? Bossier? "Math, Science, History, English—Tennis 4," the yearbook notation read.

Warren was a car nut and a work-with-his-hands kind of guy. I imagined I'd find four years of shop class and car mechanics listed in Warren's senior-yearbook notation. Why would a tennis-racquet-wielding college-prep Simpson hang out with a blue-collar wrench-turner like Warren? I thought back to the moment in Maureen and Warren's front room waiting for Mary. Did Warren say he was friends with my birth father? I gnawed at my lip. Or had I assumed they were friends because Warren said they'd hung out together?

I went into the kitchen and poured a glass of cold water from the fridge. I stared out the window into the green womb of the summer holler. Some days I felt secluded and protected in the verdant acreage—thick oak trunks, deadfall, and the underbrush of prickly brambles a vegetative fortress. Other days I felt constricted and isolated by those very same elements. I sipped the water, the taste of iron and West Virginian limestone substantial on my tongue. An unkind thought arose—Mary had been a simple girl who'd happily spent her adult years in academic food service; Simpson was a nice-looking boy bound for college. What common ground could they have had during the six months she'd said they dated?

I shrugged, then went back to the computer. Ancestry.com this time, where I found records showing William J. Simpson Jr. had joined the military in the fall of 1955. Hmmm . . . a college-prep guy joins the Army rather than the freshman class of Michigan State University? Or had he gone to college but beat feet once he learned about the burgeoning-baby-bump situation?

The non-identifying information I'd received from Catholic Charities noted that my birth mother claimed she didn't know who my birth father was. Later in the note, "talk of marriage" was mentioned, but the pastor at the parish my birth grandmother had been deeply involved with advised against it. Was it possible Mary's parents consulted with the Simpsons without Mary's knowledge? "Get out while you can. No need to ruin your lives too"? Or maybe my maternal grandparents insisted on Jack taking responsibility and his parents sent him off? Trading a shotgun wedding for military-weapons training? Better to fight for the country than for an unborn child?

Ancestry records revealed Simpson's Social Security death benefits began in August 1987. No obituaries came up. No indication of cause of death. Doing the math, he was forty-nine when he died. So young! Cancer? Heart attack? Friendly fire? *Jesus . . . another mystery. Another fuuuuucking mystery I am forced to try to solve on my own with limited and sketchy clues and a goddamn pendulum.*

After a restless night, I decided to back off from more Simpson-related research. I had circumstantial evidence—eh, not even evidence . . . conjecture, but not a single shred of proof he was my birth father. I could ask Warren and Maureen if he'd been part of their crowd, but that would mean reconnecting with them, which would mean reconnecting with Mary, which would mean agreeing to live in the secret closet.

I absolutely wanted to know the identity of my birth father, but secrecy was too big a price to pay for that knowledge, especially if Simpson had been my father. *He's dead. And not that I'd want to be in reunion if he were alive, but. . . . But what? Well, I could learn what he died from and may find some pictures of him somewhere and somehow. . . . Damn it . . . I just want to know! It's my right to know!* I didn't want to romanticize things. Just wanted the basic information I'd wanted from the beginning.

# Chapter 13

Looking around the grid of white laminate cubicles at 6:30 p.m., I saw not another soul on my side of the office. The only reason I was still working so late on a nice summer evening was the solid red line on the traffic app indicating a three-hour commute from my job in Rockville, Maryland, home to West Virginia. Waiting another fifteen or twenty minutes in the sterile confines of my government workplace for traffic to clear would cut my travel time almost in half. As I waited, I checked my phone for personal emails. Delete. Delete. Delete. *Oops, what was that last one?* I retrieved it from the trash. "Your DNA results are in!" the email subject line exclaimed. I opened it, squealed, then clicked the link to the AncestryDNA site.

A colorful pie chart on the tiny phone screen revealed my "ethnicity estimates." A map with amoebas of color overlapping like a Venn diagram zeroed in on the confluences of my ethnic mix: 37 percent Irish; 37 percent Great Britain; 16 percent Western European; 9 percent trace countries. Based on the tight cluster of overlapping colors, it was obvious my ancestors hadn't strayed much beyond the United Kingdom.

*Huh. Almost 40 percent Irish. I could definitely live with that. Kinda have to live with it. Almost 40 percent Great Britain. As in Simpson? As in William J. Simpson Jr., the dark-haired young man the pendulum identified as my birth father?* I'd once had a spiritual teacher from Ireland tell me, "Your people are from County Clare," in the West of Ireland. I was thrilled by his pronouncement, as I'd fallen in love with that area on my first trip to Ireland in my forties. I checked the AncestryDNA map; damn, the amoeba for Ireland didn't loop down that far. No Native American or Japanese amoebas either, so that didn't help in winnowing down the daddy options in the Northridge High School yearbook.

Next to the pie chart was a "DNA Matches" section, with the notation, "536 4th cousins or closer," and a "View All DNA Matches" button. It hadn't occurred to me they'd match people, but in hindsight it made perfect sense—Ancestry.com's whole deal is to facilitate genealogical search and connection. I hovered a finger over the "View All DNA Matches" button. *How many cans of worms will this open?* Shoulder shrug. Click. At the top of the display was an entry marked "Extremely Confident" that I was a first cousin or close family to "RB."

*Ohhhh shiiiiit.*

Nobody in Mary's family aside from Maureen and Warren and my two half sisters knew about me; that was the whole reason Mary needed me to remain secret. *If RB gets notified, they are for sure gonna start asking questions.*

I cradled the phone with two hands, then set it down on my cubby counter in slow-mo like it was rigged with explosives. I raked my fingers through my short crop as my mind whirled. *How does this work?* If I got notice of the match, did RB get notice too? I pecked the phone screen alive, then checked RB's status—active the day before, so if Ancestry had notified them, they wouldn't have yet received the news.

Mind whirling. Whirling. Whirling. I felt bad I'd inadvertently put Mary at risk of having her cover blown. But I also felt a little . . . okay, a lot, like, "It's your own fault, Mary . . . if you had just told me about my birth father, I wouldn't have had to spit in a tube to get matched to kin. And, by the way, you owe me $100 for the DNA test. And $55 more for the smelly and grainy yearbook."

After a long self-debate on my blessedly clear commute home, I realized I needed to alert Mary to the potential ramifications of my AncestryDNA test results.

Dear Mary,

I initiated the search for my birth parents because I'd had the desire and urgency from my youngest memory to know who I looked like. That was amplified when my first grandchild was born, and then amped to a fever pitch when my second grandchild was born—she looked so much like my son; I just had to know where those dominant looks came from.

At the most practical level, I also wanted to know of my medical history to learn if my kids, grandkids, and I needed to be aware of genetic conditions or medical issues common to my lineage.

And on an emotional level, I wanted to know the story of my conception, gestation, and birth. I wanted to know what my birth mother went through and how she came to make the choice to relinquish me. Not because I wanted to judge or condemn her—far from it—but because it's a part of my history and birthright.

I have said for years that if I could learn who my birth parents were, I would tell them to rest easy, because I had no intention or desire to show up on their doorstep; just give me a few pictures, medical history, the story, and I'd be on my way. No need to let anyone know we'd talked. No need to be included in the family. No need for further contact.

I remain respectful of your wish for me to remain a secret from your family, which is why I need to let you know that information may have inadvertently been revealed to someone close to you, or possibly someone from my birth father's family.

I did DNA testing through Ancestry.com with the hopes of finding clues to my birth father. The results matched someone and me as "close family" or first cousins. I don't know if Ancestry.com alerted them that there was a genetic match, but it's entirely possible; the mission of the site is to find and connect relatives.

I have no wish to trigger additional incidents, intentionally or unintentionally. However, I need to know about my birth father. I appreciate that it may be painful or shameful to think back on the events of 1955 and 1956, but I am asking you . . . begging you to share the details. Because it's extremely painful and shameful for me not to know of the man whose DNA I carry.

I've done research about my birth father based on the very few and vague clues I have, and have identified a possibility—Jack Simpson, aka John Simpson, aka William J. Simpson Jr. If he is the one, I have learned he is long deceased. Is he the one?

Mary, I beseech you, I implore you, and again, I BEG you to share the details I seek. Once I have them, we can close and lock the book on our relationship.

You might be thinking how can you trust me? Here's why—because I've been completely respectful of your feelings and timeline for nearly eight years. I didn't push for contact when Catholic Charities reached out to you on my behalf; I asked only for pictures and the story. When I wanted to send you pictures of my grandchildren so that you could tell me who they looked like, and learned through Catholic Charities that you were bereft with grief over John's death, I gave you time to process. A year later, when you still weren't ready, I told Catholic Charities to close my file.

It was only after my Aunt Delores had her vision and I was divinely guided to you, did I step uninvited into your world. I was very careful when I approached your home, and then later when I left voice mails—I had no idea if anyone was living with you, and I didn't want the neighbors or your potential housemates to tumble to our relationship. I reached out to your sister Maureen because I took a calculated risk that if anyone in your family would have known about your circumstances back in 1955 and 1956, it would be your older sister.

If I weren't concerned about maintaining your desire to keep the knowledge of me from your family, I would have contacted the close genetic match through Ancestry.com. Or contacted your daughter, Sharon, or many others in the family through Facebook. Or reached out by phone or mail to all of your brothers and sisters or your other daughter, Shelly. I have all that contact information, and I have not acted on it because I respect your wishes. I am asking now that you respect mine.

PLEASE, Mary, please share about my birth father and your experiences learning about me, carrying me, and giving birth. When and where were you sent away? Did your parents visit you? Did you ever see me or hold me? Did you have a loving relationship with my birth father? I know you named me Theresa Lynn—was that a family name? I know you have a sister named Theresa.

Know that the information and stories you share will

land on kind and compassionate ears and an open and gentle heart.

Thank you,
Candi

PS. You can just write me a letter or send an email. We never have to talk directly if that is your choice.

I sent the letter off to Mary the following day. A week went by with no contact from RB or Mary. I could see from RB's status they'd logged into Ancestry daily. They certainly would have seen the DNA match by this time, I thought. Maybe I'd worried myself and Mary for naught. And Mary had surely received and read the letter. I pictured her reaching into her mailbox and seeing my return address after years of no contact. Did she feel happy? Angry? Scared? I was uneasy about her reading the letter alone, but I sure didn't want to start things up with Maureen and Warren again so that Mary could feel supported during this potentially life-altering revelation. I was going through this alone . . . so could she.

∼

Ten days later, just as I was beginning to let my guard down, Ancestry alerted me to an email from RB. *Oooooffff . . . buckle up, kiddo, here we go.*

Hi Candi,
    Our DNA match shows we are a close family match, maybe 1st cousins. As far as I know I had one 1st cousin,

who died when he was about 15 years old. Do you know
how we are related?
Thanks for your help, hope to hear from you.
Ruth


Hmmm . . . not so earth-shattering. Just a curious genealogist.
No wagging or pointing fingers of blame and shame. I considered
how to respond. I hadn't heard back from Mary—was she just tired
of the whole thing? Filing a protective order? Dead? For all that I
wanted to rip off the "Hello, I exist!" bandage and put an end to the
bending to Mary's wishes, I just couldn't bring myself to risk "ruining an old lady's life."

Hi Ruth,
    You and I are related, but I'm not at liberty to say how.
Sorry to be so mysterious, but I was adopted at birth, and
my birth parent wishes our relationship to remain private.
    I know that part of the thrill of genealogy is discovering
the unknown, and I am certainly that to your family. :) May
I ask of you to maintain confidentiality please?
    I hope that someday, you and I can have an open
conversation, and that you might agree to share the results
of the genealogical work you've done.
    Thank you for reaching out to me, and for your discretion.


Kindest regards,
Candi


I got an email back from Ruth within hours.

Hi Candi,

I know who you are, but no one openly talks about it. I hesitated to contact you because I did not want to hurt you or your birth parent.

You are more than welcome to my genealogy work, sharing is what family history is all about.

Thank you for your response, I wish you all the best,


Ruth


I gaped at the screen. Reread the short note a dozen times: "I know who you are, but no one openly talks about it." What in the actual fuck? A *cousin* knows who I am? Did Mary lie to me . . . lie right to my damn face . . . that no one in her family knew about me? Maureen and Warren . . . had they lied too? It hadn't felt that way, but if a *cousin* knew. . . .


Hi Ruth,

Thank you for your thoughtful note. I appreciate your sensitivity about reaching out to me.

I wasn't sure, though I suspected, that you might be alerted to the Ancestry match. My birth parent and I have not been in touch since shortly after an unplanned reunion two years ago, but I sent a letter just last week to let them know someone might have learned of the close genetic match. I don't know what they might do with that information, but thought I should let you know I've shared the possibility with them.

I'm grateful for your generosity in sharing your family tree. From the time I was in grade school, I wanted to know my lineage—my blood lineage, though of course I hadn't those words for it at the time. Where did I come from? Who do I look like? Who are my people? And now, thanks to your hard work, I'll know part of the story.

Candi

So obsequious—I was thanking her for tiny morsels—and yet . . . I *was* genuinely grateful. *But* . . . it felt like too much work for so little too late.

Hi Candi,
Thanks for letting me know about the letter you sent, was it for someone on my side?
I want to share a bit of who I am. I am 64 years old, my husband, Steve and I live in Lansing, Michigan. We don't have any kids. Besides history and genealogy, I enjoy gardening with plants native to Michigan, a bit messy but fun, good for wildlife. Steve & I are both retired, he from banking, me from nursing.
I am happy we "met" and I was able let you know some of your story,

Blessings to you, Ruth

I thought it curious that Ruth mentioned her age. I screwed up my face like I was ciphering a difficult SAT problem. Ostensibly, I was the first child born to Mary or her siblings, so I'd be the oldest cousin. If I was sixty, and Ruth was sixty-four, we couldn't be cousins. Was that right? I sketched out boxes and arrows on a piece of scrap paper. Yep. So then Ruth had to be . . . ooooohhhhh . . . Mary's *sister*.

Hi Ruth,

I'm touched that you shared some details of your life. Creativity must run in the family—I am interested in photography, mixed-media, mosaic, and anything to do with paper crafting. There are sketch pads, colored pencils, markers, glue sticks, and glitter pots within arm's reach in most rooms of my house—as much to do with me as my two granddaughters (my son's girls), ages 5 and 7, who live nearby and come for frequent sleepovers.

A dime dropped for me last night. When you said you knew of me in a previous note, and in your latest note shared your age, I recognize we could not be cousins. I'm thinking you already knew that and wanted to let me come to that realization on my own.

My birth parent was adamant about not revealing our relationship because "no one else in the family knows." If, in fact, you and others know, then perhaps it would give my birth parent a sense of relief to know the siblings know.

Are you willing and comfortable sharing what you know about me? If not, I understand.


Thank you and all good blessings to you,
Candi


Hi Candi,

I like it we have something in common. Creativity is a trait, we like to build things too. You must be a fun Grandma!

I don't think your birth parent has gotten the letter yet, been on vacation for 2 weeks, will be home next week.

Your birth parent does not know that I know.

As with most people your birth parent has weathered

storms in life, with strength & grace, but emotional pain can come up fast as can joy & laughter.

We are a close, supportive family, and would help your parent come to terms with your birth & adoption. We would all welcome you.

I will talk with some family members, then let you know what they think.

It would be a relief to just open the windows! I hope with God's grace we can.

With love, your Aunt Ruth

This was *so* not what I expected or wanted from my little silliness with saliva. I thought another Aunt Dolores–type miracle would happen and I'd hit the William J. Simpson Jr. jackpot . . . a note from AncestryDNA—"You've got male!" I'd snoop around my paternal family tree, calculating how far apart in age I was from any other of his children. Compare my features to those in the bounty of pictures a thoughtful and thorough Simpson genealogist would have posted. Locate the great-greats' birthplace on a map. Track down obits for medical info. Dust hands. Curiosity sated.

But now there's all these Flynn family members, and windows to open, and . . . uuuuuugh.

Hi Candi,

My sister Deidre told me about you when I was in my late teens. The family was told Mary was at cooking school. Just realized that's kind of funny, bun in the oven and all. (My humor is kinda odd!) My Mom would go to see Mary at the home for unwed mothers. I wish you could have met her.

Not sure who your birth father is, hope Mary lets you know.

I opened the window. I called Sharon, Mary's daughter. I sent Sharon our emails and told her about your letter to Mary. Sharon & Shelly are going to talk to their mom.

Maybe the real reason Mary has been so secretive has more to do with the pain of giving you up than not wanting anyone to know. She took me & my younger sister Teresa under her wing after. We spent a lot of time with Mary & her family.

There is so much I would like to tell you but I am not that good about putting into words what I think.

Love, Ruth

Well didn't shit just get really real? I exhaled like I was blowing "Taps" on a dented bugle, then headed to the kitchen for a medicinal dose of wine. Cold, sweet Riesling in hand, I flumped onto the couch and swung my feet onto the low coffee table. I tilted my head back and stared up at the cedar-lined cathedral ceiling. What am I going to do with these people? I needed to talk this out with someone, but who? My family and non-adoptee friends would express empathy, love, and support, but they wouldn't . . . couldn't . . . get the . . . gut . . . of it—they could witness, but not dance with it.

Okay . . . what about the adoptees? My brother, Peter? Oh hell no. We hadn't spoken in years. If I did contact him, he'd shanghai the conversation, minimize or ignore my situation, and focus on himself—he was working nine hundred hours a week, spent another three hundred hours a week doing highly important stuff, and was utterly exhausted from walking on water.

My sister, Maggie? Maybe. I screwed up my mouth. Hmm . . . maybe not. She hears anything about adoption through her reunion and post-reunion experiences—"You're better off not knowing"; "See, now you know how I feel"; and "I can't even remember my birth mother's name." Nope, not gonna talk to her about this right now.

I leaned forward, took a sip of wine, and considered who was next on the adoptee list. Maggie's birth brother, Mike? He's a good listener, but I wasn't sure the conversation would go much beyond a single question: "Oh man, so what are you going to do?" And I'd already claimed that one.

Last option: my work bestie, Suzanne? No. She's never considered searching. I extended a jazz hand, clicked my tongue, and said, "Well, thazz all I got." I chugged the remaining Riesling, then made my way to my bedroom on slightly wobbly legs.

# Chapter 14

I popped awake in the dark and reached for my iPhone on the nightstand. Squinting, I could see it was 2:43 a.m. I laid back down, closed my eyes, and drowsily debated about getting up to pee. Ruth's words, "Sharon & Shelly are going to talk to their mom," ghosted through my brain. My eyes snapped open, and I checked the phone again. No missed calls. No texts. I hesitated, then clicked on the email icon. My eyes were sleep-sanded, making the small screen difficult to read. I blinked and widened my eyes, trying for focus as I scrolled down past several middle-of-the-night email alerts. Nestled between a Macy's three-day-sale announcement and notice of a new meditation series was the email I knew had pulled me from sleep.

Dearest Candi,

I write this letter with much gratitude and a thankful heart! Thank you Candi for not giving up and keeping your promise to your Aunt Delores!

I just got back home Sunday night and received your letter in the mail Monday. I literally finished reading your letter about an hour before Shelly and Sharon came over. I had no idea I was going to receive this letter from you but am very happy I did!

Sharon and Shelly wanted me to know that they had

spoken to my sister Ruth. And as I know now, Ruth felt this information needed to come out. Sharon was very moved and emotional when her Aunt Ruth called her Sunday morning. It was during my conversation yesterday with Sharon and Shelly that they began sharing their information with me. They told me that my siblings had known about my situation for a very long time. I had no idea that they have known!

Candi, with this being said, my first desire to keep things a "secret" but to keep in communication with you when we first met several years ago has now completely left me! Just being young and immature, I really had no idea how to handle all of this! Now that it is out in the open, I feel much relief and want to keep the door unlocked and open with you and with no secrets. I look forward to learning more about you and seeing you.

Sharon and Shelly are very much in support of you and our relationship, they were so touched and so am I at how you continued to pursue your desire for all these years to locate your birth parents and learn more about the family. All of us feel your compassion. I know you and I have felt so many many different feelings all these years. I just hope and pray you can understand where I was so long ago. I will answer your questions truly to the best of my knowledge.

I have been trying to really recall the name of your birth father but to be honest with you, that part of my life was very painful for me at the time and I honestly believe that I blocked it out so deep down. The names you had mentioned in your letter, I can't honestly tell you that it may have been one of those names, I just cannot recall, I am very very sorry! Trust me, if I should have a brief moment that the name should come back to me, I will let you know!

I think he may have gone to Northridge High School in the Detroit area. I don't really remember what town the high school was in. I wish you all the best in finding that part of the puzzle, I really do!! I will ask my siblings, the older ones if they by chance recall his name, now that I know they have known about this situation for a long time. Believe me, I wish you all the best in finding the completed circle.

*She's* sorry? *She can't* recall? *She wishes me* all the best *in finding* "*that part of the puzzle*" . . . *the part that only* she *can answer for* certain? I couldn't stomach reading the rest of the email. I dropped the phone to the floor, then wrapped my arms around my belly and sobbed. Raw, heaving sobs. I was sucked into a pillow-pounding, snot-pouring, leg-kicking cyclone of anger and grief that left me an hour later like a post-tantrum child—eyes swollen shut from crying, breathing shallowly through chapped lips, and self-soothing myself to sleep.

∼

I woke up the next morning, my eyes tender, gritty slits. I kicked the phone out of the way as I shuffled to the bathroom. Looked rough in the mirror. Took an antihistamine to unplug my cried-up sinuses. Ran cold water on a thick white washcloth to rehydrate my eyes and decrust my face. Applied a substantial layer of ChapStick and made a mental note to pop a couple of lysine tablets to ward off the inevitable cold sore certain to bloom after such an intense crying jag.

I retrieved the phone I'd booted under the easy chair in the corner of my bedroom. I had little interest in reading the rest of the email.

Who gave a damn what the flock of Flynns had to say after Mary dropped the f-bomb—the father bomb. Mary and her merry band of tight-lipped sibs couldn't or wouldn't give me the information. By holding it out of reach, they were stirring up in me an even stronger urgency to learn the truth of my paternity. Eight years ago, I'd been curious, but now I felt unfairly . . . no, *cruelly* . . . denied. For years I'd played the game Mary's way: given her home-team advantage, handicapped the score in her favor, and bowed and scraped and humbled and even humiliated myself in the process of claiming and naming my biological origins. Such an old pattern of belief—*if I were a better wife or daughter or employee, so-and-so would be a better husband or parent or boss.* In contorting myself to suit Mary, I'd lost myself.

After making the bed, vacuuming the rug . . . and the easy chair, and dusting the lampshades to distract myself, I gave way to curiosity about what else she'd said, pulled up the email, and scanned the remaining bit.

We dated for about 6 months, relationship was good at first, as time went on, he seemed to develop a very controlling, demanding, and a bossy-like personality, which I did not care for. He was somewhat tall with dark hair. We broke up due to conflicting issues and he just left, never heard from him. Candi, he was never told or knew that I was pregnant, this was the decision of my parents, I was young and they made the decisions for me. I am sorry.

Sharon and Shelly asked me if he forced himself on me, he did not, it was one of those situations where he kept pressuring me. . . . I was young and I gave in.

When I thought I may be pregnant, so scared and afraid and now I had to tell my Mom, she then had to tell my Dad. My parents decided I would have to go to a place for pregnant unwed girls about 15 miles from my home. My Mom, Grandmother, and Great-Grandmother would come to visit me throughout my stay. My parents took me there when I was about 2 1/2-months pregnant. I stayed there for the remainder of my pregnancy with you. I remember the staff being very kind and caring to us.

I shook the phone and gritted my teeth. "But you can't remember my damn birth father?!"

My parents were very caring and loving people but when I got back home, it was never brought up again, I guess that is just how it was back then. I think I just blocked so much of it out of my mind in order to process it and to deal with it. Down the road when I was older, mid 20's, I met a truly wonderful man, Martin, later to be my husband of 38 years before he passed away from prostate cancer. I have chosen not to remarry. We had a wonderful and happy life together.

My pregnancy with you had no physical or medical complications, no sickness, that I can remember, my labor went pretty well and lasted for about 6 hours. You were born with a lot of dark hair. I was able to hold you for 45 precious minutes. I was very happy to have had that moment! While I was holding you I just thought the name Terry Lynn was fitting for you, you were so adorable and beautiful.

*Seriously, you can remember holding me for forty-five minutes, but you can't recall the guy who knocked you up after dating for six months? Let's do the math here . . . that's 262,980 minutes!*

Our family is very loving, supportive, kindhearted, and fun spirited and you and your family would be a beautiful addition. We find our hope, strength, and faith in God and believe He is always here for us and with us.

Candi, I really hope I have answered a lot of your questions. Given the time it has been, it is hard to remember all details as they occurred. You have been nothing but respectful, kind, and considerate with handling questions and details and of family.

Sharon and Shelly feel your caring personality. They desire to get to know you and meet you.

Sent with Love and Hugs,
Mary

"Our family is very loving, supportive, kindhearted, and fun spirited, and you and your family would be a beautiful addition"?

Fuck. You.

Except I didn't say that . . . at least not to them. I said it to myself. Friends. Colleagues I trapped in the office kitchen or bathroom. Had it down to an elevator pitch: "I was denied details of my lineage and pictures for years because of my birth mother's fears of being judged by her family. Turns out her siblings knew all along and now they're all hearts and flowers and are ready to welcome me into the family." Emphatic expletive added when audience-appropriate. Everyone in my circles—and hapless random strangers—knew how I felt about Sharon, Shelly, and Mary's earnest and heartfelt desire to bake me back into the family mix. I told everyone . . . except the very people scootching together to make room for me.

No, for them, instead of voicing my anger and frustration . . .

I sent flowers. A pricy arrangement for each—Sharon, Shelly, Mary, and Ruth—with a card that read, "Together at last."

*Together at last? WTF, Byrne?!* Why was I encouraging them? Where was the straight shooter Candi, the one who'd been called out as "too direct" by virtually every boss I'd ever had? While I'd been pretty direct in the post-AncestryDNA plea to Mary, I mean, come on . . . there was no ambiguity in "together at last." Minor detail though: That message in no way reflected what was in my heart.

Was there an unconscious desire to highlight all they'd missed—a generous, thoughtful, and poetic woman with enough discretionary income to pony up for an extra-large arrangement? Did I secretly want to lull them into a false sense of connection then pull a trickster nanny-nanny-boo-boo move to get back at these people for all I'd been through? Or was it that I had a kind heart and didn't want to hurt them after all they'd been through?

Over the next few days, I was inundated with Facebook friend requests from Flynn kin and gushy texts from Sharon. "Can't believe it!!!!!"; "We're pinching ourselves!!!!!"; and "When can we talk?!!!!!"

Ruth sent a sweet picture of her and her husband, Steve, holding the flowers I'd sent her. I didn't feel pressured by Ruth to jump right into the family, so I asked her if we could talk. We had an easy and lovely conversation, sharing light details about our respective lives. I asked her why she'd done AncestryDNA; as the family genealogist with full access to information and records, she would have no need for biological backup. Ruth said Steve was adopted and had no clue about his lineage. He'd done it for the same reason I had. She did it as a why-the-heck-not, and to be supportive of her husband. I'm embarrassed to say I don't recall asking if they'd been successful in learning about Steve's background.

In her recounting to me of the "opening the window" conversation she'd had with Sharon and Shelly, Ruth casually mentioned that her mother, my birth grandmother, had gone to Sharon and Shelly ten years prior to her death, told them they had a sister, and implored them to find me.

I recalled sitting in Maureen and Warren's living room the day I met Mary and how she'd poleaxed us with the news that she'd told her husband and three children about me. They'd cried "like Niagara Falls," I remembered her saying, "and then it was over." I hadn't asked, but I'd imagined the three kids as being in their late teens. I wondered anew: Had they asked about finding me? It would have been easy for them—they had access to firsthand knowledge of dates and places, no Aunt Delores–type miracles required.

And then there was their grandmother . . . coming to them, forty-some years of guilt and shame weighing heavily on her mind. What triggered her fervent plea for Sharon and Shelly to find me? Why had she not come looking for me herself? Had she made the "find your sister" case to my half-brother, John, or did she only appeal to the girls? Yeah, "together at last," but no thanks to any of *them*.

Sharon continued pushing for a phone call. With my new knowledge that she'd had twenty or thirty years to initiate contact, it's no wonder she was eager to connect—to alleviate the guilt and shame she and Shelly likely carried for not taking the initiative earlier. And no wonder I was retreating and wishing for longer arms to keep them at bay. *Tell her no! Foot down. No. No way!* Except . . . "Sure. Of course. How about next Saturday?"

I felt like an old-fashioned pressure cooker, the scary kind—hissing, chattering release valve spinning atop the heavy metal lid the only indication of anything going on inside of the thick, solid pan. If too much pressure builds up, that baby will blow, spewing shrapnel indiscriminately.

*You've got to tell them how you're feeling,* I told myself over and over. *Tell them you're angry—so, so angry—about the years you've spent trying to get information and how they're glossing over—hell, ignoring—the denial. And how hurtful it was to be shut down every single time. And how frustrating that every tactic you tried for learning the most basic details about your origins was an epic fail. And most of all, how humiliated you feel having handed your power over to them in the hopes of gleaning even the most meager of informational crumbs.*

*But they'll be devastated.*

*And?*

*And . . . well . . . they obviously aren't as emotionally intelligent as I am, so they will fall apart. I'll ruin their lives, just as my son predicted, except with more collateral damage.*

A memory from a session with my former long-term therapist floated up. I'd said I felt responsible for the difficult relationship my kids had with their father: "If I hadn't left him, they'd probably have a good relationship with him now."

She had leaned forward, dark eyebrows elevated to her hairline. "Candi," she'd said in her low, Israeli-accented voice, "I hear grandiosity. You're just not that powerful to cause a negative outcome for your children, twenty years after you'd made the decision to leave your husband."

"Ruining the lives" of the Flynn clan—another example of grandiosity?

~

Maybe my former therapist could help me navigate this situation. Get me out of the shit show I'd so completely and thoroughly rolled myself in. She was happy to hear from me and intrigued by the tidbits of my birth-people saga. Open to scheduling a session, but not until she'd returned from international travel in two months. There was no time to wait; it was pretty clear from my split personality, and self-medication with alcohol, carbs, and sugar, I didn't have the tools to manage interactions with "Those People," as I'd taken to calling my birth relatives.

I found a social worker who specialized in post-adoption issues such as reunion. She was oh so young—I likely had a jar of pickles older than the long-haired blonde who ushered me into her commodious contemporary office in the DC suburbs. She gestured to a low, puffy leatherette couch. If I sat on it properly, my butt would graze the floor, eyes level with my knees. I perched on the edge, shins practically parallel to the floor, right elbow anchored to the slick arm, left hand Geigercountering for a solid stabilization point. "Are you comfortable?" Blondie inquired.

"No, but let's just go ahead."

She made the first of what would be many head tilts and facial gymnastics meant to communicate her active and compassionate listening skills. "Oh, um, yes, well then, please tell me how I can be of help."

I refrained from saying "more couch, less contraption"; instead, I sketched out the situation with Those People, then said, "So, what I need is a strategy to help me deal with them."

Blondie consulted notes on her clipboard. "So, you're feeling anger, frustration, and confusion, is that right?"

"Precisely. So what do I do about it? How have others in reunion handled this kind of thing?"

Nod. Head tilt. Facial gymnastics. "I'll need to know a little more," she said, scooping back hair from her face. "Tell me, how do you feel about not knowing the circumstances of your conception?"

Fair question. I'd wanted to know the circumstances . . . had even mentioned that in the post-AncestryDNA note to Mary. As I sat contemplating, two things occurred to me. One, how many people actually know their conception circumstances save for the standard sex-ed stuff? I had no idea of the specifics of my kids' conception. Oh I could do the math and get a general idea of when Brendan's sperm barged its way into my egg, but so what? And two, why was this important for learning about how to manage the expectations of Those People?

"Look," I said, "I've done a lot of processing about the circumstances, the situations, the why, the how, and the what. I need help dealing with the who. The who, who want to be in everlasting love and reunion. What am I supposed to do with the whos?!"

She made an "I'm genuinely compassionate and empathetic to your situation" face and said, "I'm sorry, I'm afraid we're out of time."

*Good, cuz I'm out of patience. Plus, I've lost circulation from the hips down.*

Blondie jotted an additional note on her clipboard, then asked, "Shall we book another appointment to continue our discussion?"

I levered off the edge of the sinkhole rim and onto numb and unsteady feet, tilted my head, and puckered my mouth like I'd bitten down on a kosher dill of pre-Blondie vintage. "Thanks . . . think you've helped me all you can."

∽

The first phone call with Sharon went about as I'd expected—a verbal rehash of the "can't believe it," "pinch me," "so emotional" post-AncestryDNA reveal email and subsequent texts. And my "I'm so sophisticated, super cool, funny now-I'm-the-big-sister" performance. A performance that was . . . huckstery, inauthentic . . . verging on psychopathic.

My former therapist had said that anyone who thinks they are a psychopath is too mentally healthy to actually *be* a psychopath. But how else to explain how I could, with no effort, guilt, or remorse, anticipate and calculate exactly what Sharon needed to hear and feel, while leaving anything emotionally true about myself out of the equation? I thought about those search shows on TV—*Who Do You Think You Are?* and *Long Lost Family*—and the articles I'd read about teary reunions between people separated years and lifetimes ago. People who'd never met, but due to shared blood and DNA feel the pull to each other. The missingness.

My brother, Peter, had a weepy reunion with his birth mother. My sister had her emotional introduction to her birth brothers and a raft of other relatives. She'd made a speech and presented the guys with gifts engraved with "and then there were three." What was wrong with me that I'd just as soon pull the plug and have my birth people remain long lost? Like birth mother, like daughter? For years, Mary had insisted the memory of my birth—of me—be entombed in a hermetically sealed vault. And for the memory and identity of my birth father to be torched and the ashes scattered.

Sharon called several more times, her conversation an increasingly tiresome variation on the "pinch me" theme. She noted that I seemed very calm about the amazing circumstances that had brought us together. "Ya gotta remember, I've been at this a looong time," I said, the snarky, silent subtext barely masked—*thanks to you and your family.*

She switched tactics after that and started asking getting-to-know-you questions—what kind of music did I like? Books? Movies? It felt like I was speed dating my half sister. The more persistently and determinedly she tried to get to know me, the more resistant I became. Truth be told, I was an asshole, the worst parts of me coalescing into

a complete and utter shit, rebuffing her genuine desire to make up for
lost time and learn about each other.

Shelly was clearly content to let Sharon take the lead on breaking through hard Candi. I had only one call with Shelly, an echo of
Sharon's calls, with the addition of "God is good" sprinkles. There
was a gentleness to her, almost a fragility; a laciness compared to the
heavy brocade of her twin.

As for me, I was marine-grade canvas—stiff, rough, and unyielding. I did not like this me—the regressive, petulant, reactive me;
where had the compassionate, empathetic, emotionally intelligent
me run off to? I needed that me to help navigate these new and
unexpected circumstances, not the tantrum-y, victim-y, emotional
flip-flopper who'd taken the reins of this reunion. Was I trying to
make them not like me so that they'd leave me alone? Push them
away so that they'd abandon me . . . again? So that I wouldn't have to
be the one to begin the difficult conversation that I didn't want to be
in reunion, especially with people I'd had to force into a connection
in the first place?

I had a couple of conversations with Mary and found her "can't
believe its" more palatable than those of her twin daughters. She'd
been a prisoner of a perceived family secret for sixty years—it was
part of our shared DNA. Her release from that secret was, I imagine,
like elephants suddenly unshackled after being chained for years,
unable to conceive of the freedom to move beyond the perimeter of
the chain's length. Her family had hobbled her as surely as heartless
circus owners restrain elephants. Did she carry anger toward the
eight siblings, and their respective partners, all who'd known the
secret and allowed her to bear the burden unwitnessed, unprotected,
and unsupported? Did she know she had the right to be angry with
them? *Should* be angry for the decades she'd been manacled to the

events of 1955 and 1956, unaware that every member of her "close and supportive" family had a master key that could have released her from solitary confinement?

How would her life have been different if even one of her siblings had flashed that key of freedom when Mary returned from "cooking school" instead of letting her stew alone? How would my life have been different if Mary had known all along that her brothers and sisters knew about her "bun in the oven"? Would I have felt an urge for reunion if Mary had eagerly and readily answered my questions when I'd first asked them eight years ago? Would I have had a chance to see her full face, rather than the one that was ravaged by mouth cancer from swallowing a toxic secret?

∽

Three months after Ruth had "opened the window," Sharon texted that they wanted to meet me. *Had* to meet me.

Of course they did.

*NO! NO! NO!*

"Wouldn't that be something?" I texted back.

She amped up the texts: How about if they met me halfway? Near a state park in Ohio. Google said it was almost exactly the same distance from Michigan as it was from West Virginia. Rainbow, heart, and flower emojis.

I knew her ask would only get more insistent and urgent—we were related after all; I'd certainly been relentless and then some in my efforts to get the information I'd wanted. *Okay . . . fiiiiiiine. My sister had better goddamn come with me this time, though.* I wasn't afraid or nervous to meet Sharon and Shelly, or to see Mary again, but I wasn't going three on one without backup. Plus, she owed me big time for going with her to meet her birth family.

"You're the only one who can understand what it's like to meet a birth herd," I'd said during one of my regular Saturday calls with my sister. "I really need for you to come with me." I was surprised—and delighted—Maggie, with very little hesitation, agreed to be my wing woman.

Rather than meeting Those People at the halfway point, in the confines of an inland wooded area, I insisted we meet in a small town on the shore of Lake Erie. It wasn't my favorite body of big water—its murky waters thick with industrial runoff—but a water vista was a water vista, and I needed the breathing room only a vast liquid horizon could provide me. Mary, Sharon, and Shelly acquiesced immediately to the change of venue and to staying in the Airbnb I'd found a half block from the rocky rim of Lake Erie.

Was there some part of me secretly thrilled by the control I suddenly seemed to have? Would they kowtow to my choice of restaurants? Bend to my will about activities? Might they wear matching ugly sweaters if I so directed? No. I wasn't the controlling bitch my ex-husband had often claimed I was. And ick—would I want to know that I came from such weak stock? Bad enough to learn I came from blood that could turn diabetic-sweet at the drop of a secret. Although, much as I'd hated how Mary had stonewalled me for years, I had a grudging appreciation of the willpower and fortitude it took for her to maintain over half a century of silence about me.

∾

"You're not saying much about this meeting," my sister said, swiveling in the passenger seat to face me. "Are you nervous? Excited? Or what?"

My car gobbled up a mile of Ohio toll road as I pondered her question. *How do I feel? Angry? No, not really. Happy? No. Nervous? Hell no. Really? Or are you deflecting or hiding behind false bravado?*

I scanned my body . . . no new tight places, no stomach flutters, no tension.

"I just want to go, let them adore me, and then go home," I said.

My sister laughed.

"I never wanted this," I said for the ten thousandth time. "But I let it go too far, so now I can't back out."

Well, I could, but . . . but what? Ruin an old lady's life, like my son said? Theresa Lynn Flynn Candice Cooper Byrne—ruining lives since 1955. An equal-opportunity ruiner because now there are half sisters involved. And aunts. Uncles. A mob. Jesus, I am sick to death of thinking and talking about this. I am going. And I am going with a goddamn open heart.

"All I wanted were some pictures, not a 450-mile trip across state lines to stay in a stranger's home with relative strangers. Hah, see what I did there?"

"I can't believe we're staying in the same house with them," my sister squawked, her bangled arms waving for emphasis. "It's going to be so weeeeeeeird."

I goosed the vent dial to get some fresh air flowing. "How else would you have done it?"

She pursed her lips and sniffed. "Like we did when we met my stupid family. We stayed in a hotel and met them at their house."

"Yes, but they lived nearby. We're meeting these people halfway. Are we supposed to sit in a hotel lobby for hours with them?"

She jittered her head. "It's. Just. Weeeeeeeeeird."

Hadn't seemed weird to me, maybe because I was prepared to bail out at the first sign of discomfort or request from Mary that we relive the earliest moments of my life, beginning with nursing and diaper changing. I'd read scads of adoption-related research and though rare, there's some freaky stuff that can happen in reunion on both sides of the equation—birth mothers wanting to infantilize their now-adult offspring, and adoptees wanting to crawl up between their birth mother's legs to recreate the birthing process. I'd already met Mary, of course, and she hadn't offered to rock me like Baby Huey, but there was a herd gathering in Avon Lake, Ohio, and no telling how she'd act as part of the pack.

Sharon and Shelly had offered right away to pay their share of the Airbnb rental. "We'll settle up when we're together," I'd said, because I wanted the unfettered leeway to bolt; if I took their money up front, I couldn't freely skip out the back. Full-metal-jacket control. What a joke—they've had control all along. They. Those People. The "aren't we sweet and supportive and family centered and oh gosh oh golly a swarm of lovebugs."

Mary's control? Well, let me count the ways:

She gave me away and never looked back.

She wouldn't consent to share even the most basic information with me.

She wouldn't send me pictures.

She wouldn't stay in contact with me unless I was willing to remain a secret.

She won't tell me who my birth father is.

She wants now to tell the world about me because her supportive family finally let her know they've known all along about me.

She wants my children and grandchildren to come into the fold.

And now I was driving hundreds of miles with my sister to meet with the junior varsity who were part of Mary's control team. So tired of it all. Seven years of arm wrestling and negotiating and scheming and researching and struggling. Struggling to surrender . . . to surrender the need to fill in the missing pieces of me. It was a constant, chaotic, and compelling vicious cycle—"I neeeeeeed to know"; "just let it go"; "yes, yes I can do that!"; "no, no I can't . . . I neeeeeeed to know!"

I needed the missing peace I was certain that the missing pieces of me would bring.

Let it go.

Yes!

No! I neeeeeeeed to know.

~

I'd had a long conversation with Tammy, my energy healer, about how to prepare myself for the meeting. How to bring in ritual and grounding and a goddamn full and open heart. She recommended calling in a few spiritual guides and dipping my feet into Lake Erie as a baptism and to wash away any negativity beforehand.

I pulled into a park fronting Lake Erie. No hope of "dipping" my feet into the Great Lake without a preemptory distress call to the coast guard. Waves pumped their arms and pummeled the jetty, geysers spewing twenty feet into the air. Wind assaulted a large American flag; grommets and pulleys percussed in triple time along the pole as the Stars and Stripes flipped and snapped and popped.

The car door escaped my hand and pulsed and creaked against its stops. I tacked toward the shore, thought better of it, and settled for a quick pivot in place, hasty prayers to each cardinal direction snatched from my mouth by the wild wind. *That'll have to do. Spirit, Mom, angels, whoever, or whatever—saddle up and let's get this thing done.*

Five minutes later, we pulled up next to a compact car in the driveway of the Airbnb. At the last minute, the Flynn contingent had grown from three to six. "Did they all come together in that? I know they're a close family, but I don't think they're clowns," I said.

"Nervous?" Maggie asked.

"Nope." And I wasn't.

*Is it odd that I'm not? I'd already done the scary thing showing up unannounced on Mary's doorstep years ago. I was expected today. A command performance, really. Just want to get it done and over with. They are really nice people . . . but we are virtual strangers.*

The front door of the long, low rancher opened and a slight women with cropped white hair stepped onto the porch. Maggie sucked in her breath. "Is that . . . who's that?"

"Mary's sister, Ruth . . . the window opener," I said, then took a deep breath and reached for the door handle.

"Showtime."

# Chapter 15

From our first exchange through Ancestry.com, I'd liked Ruth's personality—wry, pragmatic, and a straight shooter. She'd put no pressure on me and didn't leave the saccharine aftertaste that my half sisters did. I was glad she was the welcoming committee; maybe she'd insisted on it to avoid having the twins swarm me.

"Well, hello," I said, and pulled Ruth into a hug. We held the embrace for a moment, then I stepped back and introduced Maggie. Ruth gave Maggie a hug, then we stood like the points of a triangle, looking at each other and laughing in a "ain't this a kick in the pants" kinda way.

"I can't wait any longer!" I heard from inside. I turned and saw Sharon, who I recognized from her pictures on Facebook. She was barely five feet tall, fleshy, and beautifully attired in capris and a bright boho blouse. A mass of long dark curly hair framed her face, smooth skin belying her fifty-plus years. Blue eyes brimmed with tears. She rattled and jangled as she reached up to hug me, her stacks of bracelets shifting much like those rolling and clattering on own my arm. She bent and flexed us side to side like she was preparing to cast a fly-fishing rig.

*This is a long hug. Am I feeling anything? Bend, flex, bend, flex. Seasick? Be serious. Be in the moment. What are you feeling? Bend, flex, bend, flex. Uuum . . . maybe . . . happy for her?*

Shelly called from the sidelines, "My turn!" and came out on the crowded porch. Though Shelly had long straight blonde hair and slightly softer features, the two were obviously twins—similar clothing, jewelry, and size. Also obvious was that the three of us were sisters, even if from a different mister. We had nearly the same features— *The nose, dear god, the witchy hatchet nose.* More striking, though, was that we were all wearing bold paisley and wrists full of noisy bling. *They're twins, so it's understandable they might have similar tastes, but for all three of us to have the same aesthetic? Weeeeeeeird, as Maggie would say.*

Shelly's hug was shorter and less acrobatic than Sharon's but just as sincere. Ruth and the twins huddled around me, faces beaming with a sweet earnestness, eyes welling with tears. Again, I felt . . . nothing. *Am I shut down? Hiding from my emotions?* I glanced around at them. *No . . . I'm here because they needed to see me, touch me, make me real. I feel no kinship with these women; we have a half serving of DNA in common, but that's it.*

Waves of their love and joy crashed against me, threatening to drown me. I felt a spark of compassion—*Yes! See, you do feel!*—but a larger part of me was coldhearted, arms mentally crossed and eyebrow cocked in judgement: *You people could have found me years ago. This love bomb is meant to obliterate your guilt for leaving me outside the walls of your family compound—your "we're so supportive of each other" family who let Mary ferment for sixty years about her momentary lapse of teenage judgment. Who's the real ruiner of an old lady's life, eh?*

I looked over the heads of the weepy twins and saw Mary inside the house, glowing with joy as she gazed upon her three daughters. My heart softened as I took in her sweet face—sparkling blue eyes, distinctive nose . . . my nose . . . that was Shelly's and Sharon's too. I did a quick sweep of the lower half of Mary's face, the part disfigured by mouth cancer, and softened further at her smile. I waggled my fingers, beckoning her into the group hug.

The five of us leaned in toward each other, exchanging breath and smiles. A soft and gentle thought bubbled up: *I am in circle with my closest blood relatives aside from my kids and grandkids. I am breathing in my lineage.*

*Yeah? So?* I startled at the voice pouting in my head. *Yeah, so, indeed. They're blood, not family.* I broke the circle and reached behind me for Maggie, blocked by the moment of reunion. *Is it a reunion? With Mary, yes, but with the twins? We've never unioned, so can we re-?*

"This is my sister, Maggie." *Was I too emphatic with* my? *Or* sister? I wanted them to know Maggie was head cheerleader for Team Candi, a team they weren't qualified to play for. I led the way into the house as they warmly welcomed her. I saw the fireplace hearth was laden with at least twenty gift bags, each more beautifully embellished than the next. *Shit, I should have gotten gifts.* "You're gift enough," my energy healer had assured me when we'd talked about preparing me for the meeting.

On the other side of the great room, the dining table had been decorated in a Pinterest-quality fall theme—seasonal tablecloth, candles, gilded silk foliage, stacks of chargers topped with autumnal plates, and bright fall napkins laid out in chevrons. Snacks were artfully arranged and presented in beautiful bowls and glassware. A small layer cake sat on a pedestal, "Family Forever" piped in chocolate script atop the smooth vanilla frosting.

My heart cracked open a bit from the thought, care, and love they'd demonstrated. I looked again at the gifts, the lovely spread, and the knot of people I was related to. *It's a homecoming. An apology. Plea for forgiveness. Introduction. Initiation. Welcome home.*

*Ack! Aw.* My emotions and thoughts whirled like an emotional roulette wheel, spinning, spinning, spinning over each hot-red *ack!* and sweet black *aw*, uncertain where the ball would settle.

*Ack! Too many in the herd! It's too much! I didn't want this! You can't make me! This is all on your terms!*

*Aw. These are sweet people. They want me to be a part of their clan. They made this meeting special.*

*Ack! Fuck you, it's too little too late.*

*Aw. Thank you. Love you.*

~

Maggie and I rolled our suitcases into the en suite master bedroom. They'd assigned us that room, even placed chocolates on the pillows, while six of them—Mary; Ruth; Ruth's husband, Steve; Shelly; Sharon; and Sharon's husband, Roger—happily shared two bedrooms and one bathroom. It was unsettling that they were content sleeping tenement-style while Maggie and I were ensconced like royalty in a space twice the size as their two rooms combined. I felt pedestalized. I'd been placed on this high perch before—there's no room for movement—and learned through painful experience how long and harsh was the tumble back down to the reality of flawed human.

After freshening up, we gathered again in the great room, snacking and chatting and laughing like we were . . . well, family. Were we all trying too hard? Or was this genuine connection? Ruth suddenly sprang up out of her chair. "I can't wait any longer to give you your gifts!" She plucked one of the pretty bags from the hearth and handed it to me. I slid my hand into a bloom of tissue paper and extracted a slice of thin, slick paper. A photo. Medium close-up of a tastefully clad woman of a certain age. Silvery soft waves of hair wreathed her smiling face. Lifelines pleated her skin, evidence that the smile was frequent and genuine. I knew those lines; they mapped to my own.

"Everybody called her 'Little Grammy,'" Mary said.

*Aw. My grandmother. My lineage. Ack! My regifter. This one, right here, made Mary give me away. Made the choice to snap my tender branch right off the family tree. Forced her naive teenage daughter to handle the loss of a child alone, creating a silence so complete and profound it went septic. She'd handed her first grandchild over to strangers. Handed me right over without a fight.*

I thought about my two granddaughters, eagerly and lovingly anticipated, both whom I held within hours of their birth. I would kill before letting someone take them. I would fiercely and ferally fight to the fucking death rather than relinquish the flesh of my flesh to unknown hands.

I studied the picture, seeing the more fay characteristics Mary's sisters, Maureen and Ruth, carried. "Steve took that picture," Ruth said, pride in her husband's photography skills warming her voice. I saw no photographic evidence on the woman's face of grief, remorse, or apology—it was all unicorns and rainbows in this ersatz Walton family. The conciliatory phrase voiced by well-meaning friends popped into my head—"That's how it was done back in those days." Yes, selfish and cowardly grandparents-to-be were more concerned about societal shaming than the well-being and support of their tender kin. A fire-breathing dragon lick of anger scorched through me. My fingers tightened on the photo. I wanted to crumple it and energetically flood her with pain.

And then just as suddenly, I melted, and compassion flooded my heart, snuffing the anger instantly. I saw Little Grammy as a woman who'd had to make an excruciating choice: let her family of eleven suffer from the very real shame her neighbors, fellow parishioners, friends, and extended family would likely heap upon the children and husband she'd spent over twenty years nurturing and protecting, or relinquish her unknown and unexpected first grandchild. For the first time, I recognized she was feral too where the sanctity of her family was concerned. She did what she felt she needed to do too. I looked up from the photo toward the others. Had they seen my inner rheostat spin from rage to rationalization? Had I maintained a poker face during my silent rant or revealed my heart-on-the-sleeve girl?

"There's more," Ruth said, tapping a finger on the rim of the pretty bag.

"I need another minute," I said, and turned my attention back to the photo, searching for meaning and connection. *We share blood. We are linked through Mary.*

"She held you, you know," Mary said. "Held you a couple of times, I think."

My mouth dropped open and I goggled at her. "She . . . held me?" *Oh that changes ever . . . y . . . thing.* Compassion vaporized. My throat clogged with indictments held back only by the thinnest dam of discretion. *How? How could she give me away after she'd tucked me in the crook of her arm, gazed into blue eyes, twirled a silken curl around her finger, pressed lips upon my forehead, and inhaled my newborn scent? And how fucking dare she leave her imprint on me, then hand me to a stranger in a starched white uniform and walk away from me? How could she sleep after cradling her baby's baby, knowing she was destined to be warehoused in an orphanage, alone and unloved?*

Would a baby slated for adoption garner more or less attention from its interim caretakers? If its own mother and grandmother could give it up, doesn't that speak volumes about the worth or value of that kid? A disposable kid. A child born of shame. Born in shame.

In secret. A secret. No proud papa bustin' buttons and handing out cigars or making jokes about her not dating until she's fifty.

But maybe the caretakers lavished extra care and love on the temporary orphans. Limbo babies. Lost souls passed from hand to hand like an unappealing side dish at dinner. Mother to grandmother to nurses to social workers to foster parents and, finally, to adoptive parents. The baby, lacking connection and familial grounding, will fear her entire life when next she will be passed along to another set of strange hands. In an attempt to be wanted . . . to be loved . . . to be necessary to others . . . she'll perform. Conform. Chameleon. Give away chunks of herself.

*I can't lose my shit about this in front of these people. Maintain.* I swallowed hard against the ball of anger rising from my belly to my mouth. The petulant abandoned child resisted being reigned in. *It's their fault! Why do I have to be nice?* I took a deep breath, then reached into the bag and pulled out a sheet of paper—a copy of a handwritten recipe from a small cookbook binder. The resolution of the copy was sharp, capturing the sepia of aged paper mottled by splashes, spatters, and spills from long and frequent use. The punched holes along the left were misshapen and frayed from countless flips to this favorite treat, "Nannie's No-Bake Cookies."

"That's our grandmother's recipe," Ruth said. "Mom made these all the time. That's Mom's handwriting." What would a graphologist make of Little Grammy's handwriting? It was a fast scrawl, as if she'd taken shorthand dictation. I noticed the upper stem of the lowercase *p* looked like a spear, the top towering over every other letter. The fractional measurements were written as one number on top of the other, a horizontal line between, rather than the more familiar side-by-side numbers with an angled separator.

My mind felt like a gyroscope out of balance, tipping and

twirling and pitching and yawing. The woman who'd scribed this simple, handed-down recipe of cornflakes, coconut, and chocolate, who'd made it for her nine children, and church potlucks, and neighborhood gatherings, had sanctioned my kidnapping. *That's what they call it when a child is taken from its mother by a stranger.* "I'll have to make these sometime," I managed to say.

Ruth nodded approvingly then tapped the bag again. "One more."

*Jesusgodletthisbeoversoon.*

I reached in a final time and felt a hard bumpy lump wrapped in tissue. I pulled it out and ransomed the object inside. "It's just a cheap tchotchke of Mom's," Ruth said, "but I thought you could use it with your granddaughters when you have tea parties."

Tears slid down my cheeks as I held a blue-and-white cow-shaped ceramic creamer. I hooked my index finger under the tail handle and mimed pouring cream from the hole in its mouth. How could Ruth know this was a perfect gift? How did she know one of the first orders of business during sleepovers with my granddaughters was to have a tea party with a chunky, beehive-shaped pot, tiny sake cups, wee vintage spoons, and a small fancy bowl with sugar cubes? *This cow creamer will delight the girls. They will argue over who gets it when I'm gone.*

*This was my grandmother's, and now I'm a grandmother. This cheap tchotchke is the only tangible connection I'll ever have to her.* How pathetic to feel so touched. To be so needy for a crumb of connection. The most pathetic part of all: to accept this as the admission price for connection. Such a pattern for me. I remember saying to my son when he was a teenager, "I don't ask for much," and his immediate response—"Which is why you don't get much." Ouch. And undeniable. *Here I am boo-hooing over a dime-store whimsy as if I'd been handed a treasure chest of genealogical gold.*

And yet. . . .

*Gonna need a Dramamine if these waves of emotion keep sloshing me around.*

I tucked the creamer back into the bag and blew out a breath. *If the rest of the gift bags hold shit like this, I'll signal our secret escape word, poncho, to my sister, grab a handful of truffles from the groaning board, and head for my West bygod Virginia hills without a backward glance.*

~

We spent the rest of the evening doing family-type stuff. Ruth brought out photo albums full of pictures taken over the years at the family compound in the Upper Peninsula of Michigan. Camp Clatterhorn began as acreage in the U.P. purchased decades before. As time went by the family drilled a well, created space for travel trailers, and, eventually, built permanent structures.

As I flipped through the album, each stiff page creaking on its metal binding and crinkling from wrinkled acetate protection, I wondered how it would have been to be a part of the rituals and habitation of that land. To know the terrain, to feel the safety, security, and sacredness of land worked and inhabited by clan.

"You must come up!" they enthused. "Big family gatherings." "We always do. . . ." "We always play. . . ." Love and anger arm-wrestled in an internal and unwinnable battle. I loved these people for trying to sheepdog me into the fold, yet railed against their enthusiastic attempts. A sudden thought hit me: *They're trying to adopt me. God, I don't need another Frankenfamily.*

~

After a late breakfast the next morning at a local diner, seven of us stopped at a craft store for supplies. I'd suggested we glean rocks from the Lake Erie shore and decorate them as mementos of the reunion.

We shopped as a crowd, meandering the aisles—an unsettling experience for someone who is almost always a solo, laser-focused, get-in-and-get-out procurer.

Back at the rental house, six women bundled up against the lakefront chill, then walked to the beach access. Mary's energy, stamina, and physical strength belied her seventy-eight years. She clambered down the storm-ravaged and cattywampus wooden steps without help or concern. *An independent adventurer,* I thought, *like my mother, Delphine. Like me.* I don't know that my mother would have been friends with Mary, maybe wouldn't even have liked her, but she would have respected Mary's adventurous spirit.

I watched my kinswomen—blood kin, and heart kin—bent over, auditioning suitable rocks, then rising in triumph, treasures in hand. The mood was light and sprightly in marked contrast to the steel-colored water and pewter sky. I wanted to lose myself to the moment, to step into the present and be contented in the simple activity, but so much unprocessed emotion kept me as a remote observer.

We tucked our booty into grocery bags we'd found at the house. The weight of the rocks split the flimsy plastic, and our carefully curated collections clattered back onto the shore. I unlooped the long, wide scarf from around my neck and heaped the rocks onto the square of mottled green fabric. I wrapped the scarf tails around my hand, then wrangled and hoisted the heavy, lumpy bundle into a comfortable carrying position. The rocks shifted and threatened to escape as I climbed the crazy-house stairs up from the beach to the street. My thoughts were equally restless: *I want to go home. I need to go home. Maggie was right—being with them like this is just weeeeeeeird.*

We spent the rest of the afternoon around the dining room table painting and chatting. Sharon did her best to interview me, probing for access, posing questions she'd previously asked during our phone calls: What were my favorite movies? Books? Foods? Those People were all genuinely curious and eager to know me. I answered Sharon's questions but didn't elaborate, parrying instead. "Favorite movie? *Auntie Mame* for sure. You?"; "I like nonfiction. You?"; and "Never met a dark chocolate–covered anything I didn't like. You?"

Maggie loved that they were asking questions. She looked up from the rock she'd turned into a snowman, the tip of her paintbrush orange in readiness to apply a carrot nose. "All *this*," she said, gesturing around the table, "is how I wanted it to be when I met my birth family. Those stupid boys—my brothers—never asked me anything about myself; they just talked about their own lives."

This *might have been more meaningful to me*, I thought, *if it hadn't taken eight years to sit around a table and talk.* I'd closed the book on *this* multiple times and yet the Universe had flapped it open again and again, pages fluttering and flipping to new chapters. *There are lessons to be learned here*, I thought, *but I am apparently a very dense and reluctant student.*

～

Drying my damp, and now paintless, hands on the seat of my jeans, I walked out of the bathroom to find Ruth poking her head into the master bedroom doorway. She looked back over her shoulder, then came into the room and eased the door closed. "I want to show you something," she said, her voice low. She stepped to the bed, then laid open a manila folder.

She shuffled through a thin sheaf of printouts annotated with neat penmanship. Neon-yellow streaks stairstepped across the page on the top of the stack. "I did some research," she said without preamble. "The highlighted names are ones that appear on both our

AncestryDNA results list, so we can rule them out as being related to your birth father." Because of her genealogical expertise, I'd granted her access to my overwhelming list of nearly five hundred DNA matches.

I sat on the edge of the bed and glanced at the papers. Was my birth father in there? Had she found a Simpson I'd missed?

"I also asked the sibs," she said, "if they remembered anything about who it might have been."

I looked into her serious yet kind eyes. "And?"

"Well, one mentioned something about a guy from a family that lived nearby, but she wasn't at all certain." Ruth shifted from foot to foot uneasily, patted her cropped white hair, then launched into a story she'd heard from one of her older sisters, Deidre. A traveling carnival was in town and an excited Deidre had asked her parents for permission to go. Their father said no immediately. Deidre had pressed the issue, asking why not. "She said Dad said something like, 'It happened to one daughter, I'm not going to let it happen to another!'"

I leaned forward, the mattress creaking beneath me. "So, you're telling me," I said, head thrust forward like a turtle, "that my birth father could have been . . . a carnie?" She shrugged and nodded.

I rocked back, clapping my hands and howling with laughter. She looked at me in alarm, clearly not expecting that kind of reaction to her news. I hee-hawed, then coughed, slapping at my chest till I could choke out between guffaws that she *had* to recount the story to Maggie, *immediately*.

Ruth left, then returned with Maggie in tow. I fanned the air with the back of my hand, gesturing for Ruth to tell the tale. "A carnie, can you believe it?" I said once Ruth reprised the anecdote. "Sure explains my love for food on a stick!" I said.

Maggie and I erupted into sustained laughter, much to the puzzlement of Ruth. I sniffed and caught my breath. "You couldn't know, but Maggie's worst fear about finding her birth people was that they'd be . . . carnies!"

Ruth waited patiently as Maggie and I wound down, gales of laughter tapering to snorts and giggles. She gathered her research papers, scattered from our hysterical outburst, then closed the manila folder. "None of the family recalled Jack Simpson," Ruth said. "Can you tell me why you think it might be him?"

Maggie and I exchanged glances. Show-and-tell time. I shrugged then pulled out my pendulum and the Northridge High School Class of 1954 yearbook. I turned my head away and had my sister flip the yearbook pages so that the pendulum couldn't read an unconscious positive response from me. The pendulum swung no, no, no until the page with Jack Simpson, where the undeniable yeses led to him.

We looked at her expectantly. Ruth's face as she observed the prognostications would have earned her a seat at the final table of any Texas Hold'em poker tournament. "I can show you how to cross-reference possible DNA matches," she said finally.

Click.

And just like that, in the master bedroom of a rented house in Avon Lake, Ohio, down the hallway from the woman who'd lain with a bossy boy—or possibly an itinerant carnival worker—in the dog days of the summer of 1955, I closed and locked an emotional door. No anger. No drama. No mental exclamation points. Just a quiet, sober, adulty moment of gut-certain choice.

*I choose no. No more of these people. No need to learn about my birth father. Just . . . no.*

∾

The next morning, Sharon and Shelly pulled me aside into the kitchen. Sharon laid her hand on my arm, our bangles chiming in unison. She looked up at me, her blue eyes wide and serious. "Shelly, Aunt Ruth, and I *really* want you to get the answers you need from Mom about your birth father, so we told her you'd like to talk with her privately before we leave today."

The familiar burn of anger flared, then dialed down to a barely tepid *ugh, whatever.* I'd resigned myself to Mary's buried memories, to not knowing who'd sired me. Now that her secret pregnancy was no longer a secret to her family—had, as it turned out, never *been* a secret—she was safe in the herd. No one other than me had pushed for answers about my paternity. They'd protect her as they always had.

I'd proven over the previous eight years that I wasn't going to out her, threaten her, or intentionally harm her. She'd proven she could hold in a secret to the point of facial disfiguration. What did they hope a half-hour private chat would reveal. Oy.

"Mary, wanna go for a walk before we have to take off?" I asked as she rolled her overnight bag past the kitchen doorway.

"Sure," she said without hesitation, abandoning the small suitcase then hurrying down the hall to get her coat. Sharon and Shelly gave me meaningful looks, eyes widened, heads nodding, lips pursed— *See how we're helping our sister? We done good, right?* I stretched a smile and raised eyebrows in acknowledgment.

∾

Mary and I stepped out into the chilly October morning, hunching our shoulders against the bullying winds as we walked along the sidewalk. Halfway to the lakefront, I halted, then touched the sleeve of her blue corduroy barn coat. We turned to face each other.

*What can I say that I haven't already said?* I took a breath. "Mary, I know that Sharon, Shelly, and Ruth said I wanted to talk to you about my birth father." She nodded once. I looked into the pale blue eyes that would be my eyes in another twenty years. Took in the fleshy, generous ears that mirrored mine. Reflected about how very white my hair would turn. "I want to say it's okay if you don't remember what happened back then." I felt her body soften with relief under my hand.

Her eyes shimmered behind her glasses. "I really don't remember—"

She stopped as I gently squeezed her arm to signal a "let me finish." "You'll remember about my birth father when and if the time is right." I shifted, my hand still on her arm. "We haven't talked about why you might not feel safe telling me." I felt her arm tense. "We've talked a lot about all that had to come together before we were re-reunited." Her eyes brightened and she nodded vigorously. "What we haven't talked about is how I disappeared after meeting you at Maureen and Warren's house."

Her gaze dropped. She took a couple of steps down the sidewalk and launched into the oft-recounted "didn't know the family knew so she needed us to remain a secret" story. I let her finish the narrative, then said, "I carry shame for not telling you how I really felt at the time. I just left you hanging and wondering." I took her hand and looked into her eyes. "I want you to know that I can appreciate how you might not trust me, consciously or unconsciously." I swung our hands. "Your memories of that time are buried deep. It's unlikely they'll surface until you feel safe and can trust me."

She did not acknowledge my statement. "I've been thinking, really trying to remember," she said, "but it was such an awful and depressing time for me."

*Ah . . . she's not ready, may never be ready to acknowledge the hurt I must have caused her.*

"I came home after being away for so long and no one said anything. So neither did I. I was supposed to be at a cooking school, and nobody even asked me to make dinner!" The wind from the lake tussled with my scarf, and I gave it a second wrap around my neck and tucked in the tails.

"I was really angry at your dad," Mary said. My mental eyes widened in surprise. *Dad? When and why would he have been in contact with her, and why hadn't he said anything?!*

"He'd disappeared. Just was gone when I got back, and I never knew what happened." *Oh, that guy.* I'd always referred to him in the formal, birth-father way, not the familiar, watched-you-grow-up dad kinda way.

I snagged her coat sleeve. "I did some research, and Jack Simpson, the guy I think was my birth father, joined the Army in the fall of 1955. The timing aligns."

Mary nodded. "You know, I'm pretty sure your dad had dark brown hair, not black. Does that help? You know, with the DNA stuff you got?"

A wave of tenderness washed through me. *Bless her heart. This dear woman is offering me all she can. She thinks I can plug his hair color into the DNA machine and out will pop my pop.* I gave her a big smile and pulled her into a hug. "Thanks! I wish it worked that way." I gestured toward the rental house. "Ready to go back?"

Mary went in the front door just as Sharon came out of the garage. Sharon's eyes searched my face. "Did she . . . did you . . . was it. . . ."

I interrupted her dithering. "She says she doesn't remember. I told her that was okay." Sharon studied my face, then flung her arms around me, hugging and rocking. *Well bless her heart too; they're all trying to make it right. Too bad it's too little, too late.*

We took pictures in the front yard of every combination of people, on multiple devices. Someone asked for a video of Mary and me, and we spontaneously reached for each other's hands and did a slo-mo skip down the sidewalk, turning our heads to look at each other, goofy grins on our mugs. Love for this woman bubbled up in me, sweet and warm, as daughter ham bone mirrored mother ham bone. The love bubbles shimmered then popped under the pinprick of the reality of the circumstances. It would have been such a different life if she'd kept me.

I was so glad she hadn't.

~

On the drive back, my sister and I dissected and analyzed the events of the weekend. No denying they were nice people. Thoughtful people. Easy to talk to and be with. "When you were out with Mary, those girls asked me if I thought you'd say in touch with them," Maggie said.

I glanced in the rearview mirror, then signaled a lane change. "And what did you say?"

She sipped at a vanilla latte. "I told them I didn't know. I said they should take it slow and see what happens." She sat up straighter and tilted her head. "I also told them I was your first sister, and that they would never replace me."

I chuckled and looked over at my first sister . . . my first child. She pursed her lips and widened her eyes in mock anger.

"Fuckin' A. You're my *only* sister, sistah."

# Chapter 16

hristmas morning crept in as slowly as it had when I was a child, but with none of the excitement. Instead, I felt dread. Ugh. Those People. I said I'd talk to Those People today. I levered myself out of bed. Hips, knees, ankles popped and crackled in concert with the floorboards, a painful and audible reminder of the twenty pounds I'd packed on since the birth-people incursion five months earlier. Merry friggin' Christmas.

I pulled on my favorite flannel lounger, the cotton thick, soft, and holding the scent of Mountain Breeze Bounce sheets, then went downstairs. It would be an hour or so before the sun rose high enough to illuminate the acres of bare trees in my West Virginia holler. At this time of year, there was a two-minute window when the rising sun cast a rosy glow over the forest. I asked myself each morning, "Would you call that color coral . . . salmon . . . mackerel . . . flamingo?" During sleepovers, my granddaughters and I snuggle close under the down comforter to wait and watch with wonder for what the girls called "pinky trees."

I plugged in the four-foot-tall fuchsia-colored Christmas tree then lit a balsam-scented candle to lend an air of legitimacy to the peewee pretend pine. I missed having a real tree but absolutely did not miss the red welts on my forearms from wrestling the tree into the holder or wrapping lights around the trunk and branches. Nor did I miss feeling hurt from the utter lack of interest in my evergreen efforts by my two children and then-husband.

Our family of eight had gathered the previous day at my daughter's house to celebrate Christmas. Our holiday tradition is to be non-traditional—there's no pressure to have things a certain way or on a specific day. As children of a firefighter whose work schedule did not always allow for family festivities to occur on the prescribed holidays, my kids are laissez-faire about when, where, and how we get together. There's a freedom in that approach, but it doesn't foster the enduring rituals I crave.

I knew from previous conversations with Those People that Christmas was their favorite holiday. I suspected they'd be over-the-top holiday decorators, from a massive real tree bedecked with ornaments of sentimental value to motion-activated dancing Santas to reindeer-shaped soap in the bathroom.

This year, they wanted to add me as a holiday collectible. "It will be our first Christmas!" Mary, Sharon, and Shelly had caroled during a FaceTime call on Thanksgiving. My gut seized at the specter of years of sappy, superficial, and artificial connections. I'd nodded my head and stretched the corners of my mouth into the kind of smile you give the dentist when they want to check your bite, and thought, *god, will this mean gifts? Chirpy cheer penned into a cutesy card or, worse, a preachy "Jesus is the reason for the season"? And it's only a matter of time before they lobby for a Christmas visit.*

Sharon had panned the phone around their Thanksgiving gathering, holding my visage up for all to see . . . The Candi Show. Dozens of strangers grinned and waved and greeted me with hearty howdys that, were I among them, would devolve to an extended discussion of the weather because we had no other common ground. I knew I'd be featured in Mary, Shelly, and Sharon's "what are you thankful for" portion of their Thanksgiving celebration. The three had said count-less times how very thankful and amazed they were that we'd found each other. I didn't doubt their sincerity. I'd received several dozen emoji-illustrated texts with that heartfelt sentiment. I'd experienced their hugs and tearful declarations of relief and joy and love during our Lake Erie reunion.

My Flynn clanswomen I'd laid eyes on, and the men who'd mar-ried into the clan, and the far-flung kinfolk who'd friended me on Facebook because I was now on Team Flynn . . . I couldn't deny they were sweet. Welcoming. Thrilled to have me back in the fold.

*How do I shut this down without grinding their fairy tale under the sole of my big black bitch boot?*

"Our first Christmas," I grumbled as I fumbled with the cof-fee-pod storage drawer, a misfit Breakfast Blend preventing full access. I strong-armed the drawer, causing two dozen environmen-tally unfriendly pods to cascade to the floor.

*Here's what I'd like to say to you on our first Christmas:*

*Go fuck yourselves, you weak, shame-ridden sheep. For years you've had the knowledge and means to find me.*

*It took me eight years of persistence—bullheaded, head banging against the wall, banging on doors, doors opened only by the grace of God—for* me *to find* you.

*Mary, I shape-shifted and soul-shifted to squeeze and contort and chameleon myself to accommodate your comfort level, and still you've denied me the chance to solve, resolve, and absolve the mystery of my origins.*

*Where I held curiosity and mystery, you held secrets. I've had com-passion all along for you, the terrified teen who was culled and sent away, wrongly shamed to avoid your parents' "What will the neighbors think?"*

*But you're an adult who's made me beg for the smallest scraps of information. I've spent hundreds of hours and thousands of dollars over almost a decade to learn what you could have provided me in thirty minutes for free. And you expect me to join your kumbaya cult because you now know your loving and supportive family—the same loving and supportive family that let you marinate in toxic silence for decades by the way—doesn't judge you? Oh, and worst of all, you wish me all good luck in finding out who my birth father is because you don't remember?*

My mental soliloquy hit a high note that made my brain ache.

"Stop," I said out loud, and opened the fridge. After yesterday's family repast, we'd packed the excess Christmas food for a fireman's family sitting vigil at a DC hospital, so there were no yummy leftovers for Christmas breakfast. I had my choice of cheese sticks, a flabby grapefruit, and ten bags of frozen brussels sprouts in various stages of freezer burn. Ehhhh. Later.

The day loomed large. Family and friends were busy. I had a metric ton of books waiting for an attentive reader. Nah. Five hundred dollars' worth of unopened mixed-media art supplies waiting for creative hands. Meh. Two clutter-filled rooms waiting for my inner Marie Kondo to appear. Uuhck.

The impending call with Those People commandeered my focus.

I eased myself onto my knees in front of the wood-burning fireplace insert I'd U-Hauled from New Jersey to West Virginia, white-knuckling the corrugated Pennsylvania Turnpike, certain the potholes would dislodge the trailer from the hitch. *Worth it*, I thought every time flames glowed in the beautiful hearth.

Once the jiffy log caught fire, I plopped on the overstuffed couch and arranged three squashy pillows to support my flame-gazing position. One minute later, I was replumping and pummeling the down squares. A minute after that, I threw the pillows on the floor. Thirty seconds later, I got up and gave up the notion of meditating on the fire to soothe myself.

Sharon had said she'd text me around one o'clock when she, Mary, and Shelly were ready for our Christmas Skype. By noon, I could think of nothing other than the call. They'd want me to gush over the presents they'd sent, but I hadn't even opened the shipping boxes they'd been mailed in. I'd just thrown them into a corner of the dining room in the space between the baker's cabinet and the wall, where they were undoubtedly messing with my feng shui. The text came at 12:45, all hearts, flowers, and smiley emojis: "We're ready!!!!! Are you ready?!"

My arms spasmed. Jaw clenched. I shook my head so vigorously that my vision blurred. *No, I am not ready. Don't want to be ready. Will never be ready.* I turned off the phone. Lay on the couch, nose to the cushions, my back to the fire. Dark. Hiding. Cocooned.

I startled awake, lifted my head, and squinted out the window. It was still daylight but not for long, judging by the position of the sun teetering on the ridge of the mountain. I tucked my head back down, wanting to shelter in place until Those People got the hint and left me alone.

Two breaths later I opened my eyes. "What the hell are you doing?" I said, my voice muffled as I spoke into the cushions. I sat up, then shrugged shoulders to earlobes. *Is this how you want to live your life? Like Maggie? Hiding and hoping they'll go away? Where are your boundaries?*

I watched the embers in the fireplace breathe cherry to maroon, cherry to maroon. *If you'd been honest with them and yourself when things broke open after AncestryDNA matched you and Ruth, you wouldn't be hibernating and hiding out from well-meaning folk.*

A recent conversation with a spiritual advisor came to mind. I'd shared with her my growing resentment over the assault of Those People. "I never wanted to be in reunion," I'd told her, "but because I'd allowed it, I didn't know how to end it without hurting their feelings."

"I've got news for you," she'd said. "Their feelings are already hurt because you're not acting like the person they need you to be."

A log shifted, and a spray of sparks bloomed and faded. *I should have ripped the Band-Aid off right away*, I thought, not for the first time . . . not even the hundredth time. And the familiar response, *Yeah, but you didn't, so now what? You do it now, and they'll be devastated.*

A tiny little voice in my mind, a new voice, raised its hand, then said, *It's not up to you to make up for the choices they've made in their lives.*

I nodded, slowly . . . tentatively . . . then faster . . . with conviction. I stood and stretched. It was fully dark now, the holler tucked in for the night. Ignoring my growling tummy, I sat at my desk and flipped open the laptop.

I scrolled through emails until I found the note from Sharon that she, Mary, and Shelly coauthored the night in July when Mary had learned her teen pregnancy was very old news to her family. The note that said we could finally be in touch because there was no longer a need for secrecy. The note that said Mary didn't remember who my birth father was and that she had no intention of remembering.

I hit reply, then chewed the inside of my cheek before writing:

Dear Sharon,
     The feeling of overwhelm around my reunion with all of you has been building up in me for some time and I must

address it. I haven't before now, because I haven't wanted to cause hurt feelings or disappointment. As a wise woman recently suggested, y'all were probably feeling hurt or disappointed anyway since I suspect you have a different idea of what a relationship with a newfound sister should feel like, rather than what your experience of me has been.

I am one person . . . you are many. You were raised in a close extended family of many and are comfortable and familiar with life in and as a crowd. My family was not that way. I can count on one hand the number of times I saw my aunts, uncles, and cousins. I can count on one finger the time my sister's, brother's, and my family have gotten together.

It was a real stretch to my comfort level to meet the group of you in Ohio. I hasten to add that y'all are super nice and extremely thoughtful and that it was a fun and easy time. You may recall from my fateful letter to Mary that when I started my search, I had no desire for reunion; I simply wanted to know my lineage and medical history and see some pictures. I showed up on Mary's doorstep not because I wanted to, but because it was the only option left open to me after years of being denied my requests for history and photos. You also know that at the end of that doorstep meeting, Mary wished to stay in contact with me, but only if I was willing to remain a secret. After a few weeks of consideration, I just couldn't agree to those terms, even though I knew it would mean cutting off any hope of learning about my birth father.

Fast-forward two years to this past July . . . AncestryDNA . . . Ruth . . . guess what, I wasn't a secret. All is well, all is in the open, and then . . . the expectation that we live happily ever after. What I failed to recognize in the days following

Ruth's "opening the window" was that my maternal pattern kicked in, and I was more concerned about taking care of Shelly's, Mary's, and your feelings than my own. About a month in, I realized I felt a white-hot anger—after years of patiently, respectfully, doggedly requesting information and pictures on Mary's terms, there was a 180-degree pivot on her part and a big ole welcome mat, no harm no foul . . . still on Mary's terms . . . and now, in addition, on the family's terms. We jumped right over my hurt, frustration, and anguish of sixty years of denial, into the Flynn lovefest.

I take responsibility for sending mixed messages. I feel conflicted, so it's no surprise that comes through. I've gained twenty pounds since we first connected in July, and I know it's from stuffing down my emotions. Please know that I am in NO way suggesting anyone other than me is responsible for my state of mind or body. Reunion is fraught with emotion—both good and bad—which is why I think I never wanted to experience it. It was easier to remain at a distance; as I've often said, I wanted the stories and pictures of my birth people, but not the actual people. I say that not to be harsh or mean, but as illumination of my mindset.

I need to say that I don't have the emotional energy to work on building a relationship with the family. I just don't have it to give. I'm sorry that I haven't shared my feelings before now, and sorry for any hurt or disappointment you may have experienced from my not sharing.

I've struggled for an hour about how to end this note. I will simply say, take good care.

Candi

I reread the note, then paused to bless Those People before hitting the send button. Sawooosh . . . off it went. I took a deep breath, palmed the laptop lid closed, then headed to the kitchen for a celebratory cheese stick.

# Part Three

*The quest for specific knowledge has caused me to stumble on knowledge of a different kind.*

—Rod McKuen, Finding My Father:
One Man's Search for Identity

# Chapter 17

A year after ghosting Those People, my two granddaughters and I were on the way back to their house after spending the day in bedlam, aka a children's museum in Winchester, Virginia. I'd planned our return trip so the three of us could view the rise of the supermoon of 2017 together.

In the back seat of my Subaru, Jillian, the six-year-old, was immersed in one of the dozens of kid-oriented apps on my phone, seemingly oblivious to her surroundings. Corrina, the eight-year-old, sat perched on a booster seat, long slender legs crossed with a poise and ease I'd never experienced in my life.

"Look to the right, girls!" I said, pointing toward the eastern horizon, where an enormous orb the color of ancient parchment was ascending. "Look at that gorgeous moon!"

"It looks like cheese," Jillian said, before going back to swiping and tapping my phone, causing whirs and repetitive music ideally suited for breaking down hostage takers.

Corrina *uh-huh*ed about the moon, then continued our conversation about her "favorite thing in life"—family. We talked about Daddy—my son—as a little boy and had a good laugh over Corrina's imitation of my sister's voice, so high-pitched we refer to her as Aunt Squeaky.

"Grandma B? Your other sisters, your birth sisters, are they my aunts too?"

The question caught me off guard. "Well they would be Daddy's aunts, so they'd be your great-aunts."

I flicked a glance in the rearview mirror and saw her nodding.

"And your birth mommy, what would she be to me?"

*Nothing. They're all nothing to you.* I cleared my throat and shifted in my seat. "Let's see—she's my birth mother, which would make her Daddy's grandmother, which would make her what?"

"Great-Grandma? Like Great-Grandma Rose?" she said, referring to my daughter-in-law's lively eighty-something grandmother.

"Yes, indeedy."

"What's her name?"

"Mary."

"So, I'd call her Great-Grandma Mary?"

"Yep."

Several mile-marker posts flashed by. The big cheese moon was taking on a milkier glow. Bleeps, bloops, and chirps from Jillian's game chipped away at my sanity.

"Is she old like Great-Grandma Rose?" Corrina asked.

"She's a little younger . . . maybe seventy-eight or seventy-nine."

"How old are you, Grandma B?"

"Sixty-one."

She processed that a moment before asking, "So, how old was Great-Grandma Mary when she had you?"

"Seventeen."

"What?" Corrina exclaimed. "That's way too young to have a baby!"

I chuckled at her incredulity. "I know. That's why she gave me to my mommy and daddy."

"How did she know them?"

Another surprising question. I shook my head and lifted a hand from the steering wheel. "She didn't know them."

"So, they were *strangers* to each other?" Corrina asked, her voice rising in shock.

I nodded. "Yep."

"Why didn't she give you to someone in her family so she could see you whenever she wanted to?" Corrina asked in disbelief.

Tears threatened to erupt. I swallowed hard to choke down a golf ball of emotion. "That would have been a good idea, right?"

She leaned forward. "Yeah, then she could have seen you and taken you back when those sisters were born so you could have grown up together!"

"That seems like it would make more sense, huh?"

She leaned back and crossed her arms. "I would *never* give my baby to strangers!"

"I know that's right!" I said, pressing a pinky to the corner of my eye to staunch tears. We crossed the West Virginia state line. "We'll be home in just a little bit, girls."

"What kind of blood do you have, Grandma B?" Corrina asked.

I'd shared the results from AncestryDNA with them, so I said, "Irish and British—remember I showed you the map I got?"

"Oh yeah! I'm glad I know more about my ancestry."

I chuckled, my mood lifted by her vocabulary. "How do you know the word *ancestry*?"

"I just do."

"Well, it's the exact right word!"

"Once I know about all the places I have ancestry, I want to go visit them."

"That sounds like a fun trip!"

"Blood from different countries tastes different," Corrina said with authority.

"I did not know that."

"Yeah, like when you're Italian and you bite your lip, it tastes different than if you're Irish and bite your lip."

Minutes later, we pulled into my son's driveway—the only home the girls have ever known. By the time I was Corrina's age, I'd had a half-dozen addresses, not counting the orphanage. My son came out to greet us and lend a hand hauling in suitcases, treasures, and artwork claimed or created over the past twenty-four hours. After a brief chat, and hugs, kisses, and declarations of love exchanged all around, I put the Subaru into gear and headed for home.

I took the back roads, animals visible in the open fields under the full moon's spotlight. I easily slalomed the curves and potholes, muscle memory kicking in as I navigated the familiar byway. I mused that I'd lived quite literally over the river and through the woods from my son and his family for eight years. Scanning my mental address book of the thirty-plus places I'd lived, I realized with a start that I'd been in my current home longer than any other in my life.

The Subaru labored up the mountain, shucking and jiving across the ruts and grooves of the bluestone driveway. I pulled up to the front of the house, turned off the engine, then tilted my head back to look out the aptly named moonroof. The brilliant orb pinned to the heavens beamed bright light into the holler, a personal nightlight. Looking to the sky, I replayed my conversation with Corrina. *Why didn't she give you to someone in her family? I would* never *give my baby to strangers.* I'd started my quest for answers because I had questions triggered by my granddaughters' births—where did we come from, who do we look like, are there medical conditions we need to worry about?

I reached for the door handle, then paused. *Really, though, no one other than me cares in the least.* My kids know who their people are, at least the people who count. My parents and my mother-in-law would always be their only grandparents. My siblings and their father's siblings would always be their only aunts and uncles. They were the only relatives they knew, the only ones whose stories they knew. Or cared to know.

With AncestryDNA, I'd received the full picture of where we'd come from. In reunion, I'd seen other people who looked enough like me—and therefore my offspring—to satisfy my curiosity. From the birth-people stories, I knew there was longevity and mental acuity into elderhood. *But it's still only half the picture.*

I bundled purse, mail, and phone under my arm, snagged a half-melted frozen fruity drink from the cup holder, then hip-checked the car door closed. Corrina, whose favorite thing in the world is family, had expressed zero interest in meeting Those People. No wonder; they weren't her people. *They aren't even* my *people.*

I dumped my load onto the dining room table, sending a slew of mail and magazines to the floor. With a sigh, I bent to retrieve the mess. The whole birth-people thing had been a mess from the beginning, each sticky step leading to an even stickier situation, until before I knew it, I was up to my neck in quicksand—an all-consuming, restrictive, and suffocating morass of anger and frustration compounded by the bone-deep need to know myself. Or what I thought I needed to know to know myself.

Papers and periodicals in hand, I eased upward, my back telling me tales of woe. My gaze landed on the picture of my mother I kept tucked under the lip of the dining room window frame. I realized with a start that she was likely close to my age in that photo. She's seated crisscross applesauce on a rug in a holy building in god knows what country. By that point in her life, she'd been to at least two hundred countries; by the time she died, she'd been to all but nine countries in the world. What had driven her to roam the globe, to risk being smuggled into unfriendly countries, to leap from a Zodiac boat struggling in wild seas to the icy landscape of Antarctica . . . three times?

Why hadn't I asked her that? Why hadn't I asked so many more things? For details about so many more things? I knew broad strokes about her life, but not the full stories. Why hadn't I probed for the specifics about her multiple husbands? About her experiences as a pilot flying small planes to pre–World War II Cuba? About finding her father dead on the kitchen floor on the Christmas morning when she was six years old? I'd spent almost a decade looking for answers from the birth people . . . why hadn't I given that same attention to my own mother?

My eyes welled, and I leaned closer to the photo and lamented as I had hundreds of times since her death, "I'm so sorry, Mom. I'm so, so sorry we didn't get it right in this lifetime."

I stood up and palmed away tears. "At least we're getting along now though, right?"

In the years since her death, and especially after her appearance in Aunt Delores's vision, I'd come to rely on . . . maybe even depend on Mom for support and wisdom, sending signs and messages from the beyond. Wishful thinking? Woo-woo? It would likely be perceived that way by others. To me, there'd been too many coincidences, synchronicities, and miracles to deny her as a benevolent and otherworldly force.

# Chapter 18

"Well, here we are, ladies and gent, Corcomroe Abbey," Fred, our laconic tour-coach driver said. "Was built in the twelfth century, though maybe later."

I'm not a fan of group tours. I don't like being part of a crowd going to places tour leaders had decided were important or worthy of seeing. This trip was different, though. What had drawn me in was the idea being in Ireland—specifically the Wehssssst of Ireland, as John O'Donohue, one of my favorite poets, would say, his musical lilt emphasizing and elongating *West*; I heard it as an exhalation of honor and reverence for his beloved Ireland.

The retreat had been billed as an elemental experience of Ireland—"Earth, Sea, & Sky"—and was led by a woman who'd spent a year in this part of the country, learning to listen to how the land spoke. The intent of the retreat was to visit sacred spots and holy wells and to hear what the land might tell us.

I looked out the windshield at the looming edifice as my fellow land lovers alighted from the coach. I'd been excited to see the abbey, knowing that John O'Donohue had held a dawn Easter service here for years. Pewter limestone blocks quarried from the local Burren landscape, rough-hewn edges blackened with age, formed the rectangular shell of the abbey. The roof had long been sacrificed to time and the elements. Dozens of Celtic crosses, some taller than my five foot five and change, crowded together in the churchyard, penned in by a low stone wall.

A steel-colored sky reflected the solemnity and soberness of this particular building. Our group of fourteen was unusually quiet as we made our way single file through a break in a stone wall, then headed to the entrance of the abbey. I ducked through the low portal into the nave and felt the energy shift. Though the space was open to the sky, I felt confined. Restricted. The retreat leader read a passage penned by John O'Donohue, but I couldn't focus on the sentiment. My pulse quickened. Breath moved from my belly up to my chest. I needed to move, to stir up the heavy energy. The floor was carpeted with grave markers, four- and five-foot-long slabs of grainy, lichened limestone. Names and dates had faded and softened into barely discernible dimples. It felt wrong to trample on these people, to tread upon their spirits, to view them as thousands and perhaps millions of visitors had—as stepping-stones to another tourist site. Pictures to be taken. A box checked off.

I nodded to my fellow travelers as we looked up between hopscotching the narrow grass paths fringing these sacred oblongs. Quiet . . . we were so quiet . . . not our usual lively and chattery selves. I looked to the front of the church to the empty windows, where I imagined ornate stained-glass panels once provided color to this somber space. I inched around a person in my group who seemed frozen in place and headed for a spot in the corner of the building free of the horizontal grave markers.

Though the abbey was aboveground, the niche felt subterranean— solid walls on three sides with a small window perhaps the size of the cement block the only source of light and circulation in this corner of the building. I could smell the limestone weeping . . . dampening the hard-packed earthen floor. I started to shake. That smell. The shadowy corners. The small window. I felt myself being transported to a previous lifetime—a lifetime that had been revealing itself to me in visual snippets and visceral reactions for several years. A lifetime where I'd been placed in the dungeon for speaking out. For speaking my truth. My voice . . . and my very being . . . meant to be buried alive as punishment for speaking truth to power. I looked up at that small portal and knew in that lifetime, I had been in a place like this. Very deliberately placed where I could see the sky . . . the sun . . . the moon. Where I could see the freedom that was out there . . . but not for me. I'd been locked away with no way out.

My breath came as quick pants. My eyes streamed tears. *No way out no way out no way out.* I jerked around, needing to get out of that space. As I turned I saw two iron rings embedded in the wall. Shackles. I'd been shackled in that place. *No way out no way out no way out.* Panting. Sobbing. Gut clenching. *NO! I am the way out. That was then. I am* free.

I stumbled from the corner past the woman still frozen in place. Who knows how long we'd been in our respective states of altered consciousness . . . seconds? Minutes? I made my way to the far side of the abbey, silently begging forgiveness of the dead I trod upon to reach the safety of life outside those walls.

The heavy energy lifted as I left the interior; light earthy energy bathed me. I took in the verdant landscape—low green-napped hills studded with leggy shrubs. I saw a lone hawthorn tree—a fairy tree—crowning the modest vegetation at its roots. My breathing slowed, and I swabbed at my face and leaky nose with a scrap of tissue I'd found in my jacket pocket. I felt myself being revivified by the natural surroundings. Shook my head. *What the fuck happened back there?*

I noticed my retreat roommate pressed up against the abbey, head tilted back, a most beatific smile on her face as her artist eye took in the crenellations and colors of the limestone. I knew the stone was speaking to her. And I felt in my gut the limestone had something else to say to me.

The day before, a Yoda-like man had taken us on a hike through the ripples and ridges of the Burren, the lunar-looking area of County Clare where our retreat house was located. He'd said limestone was created from the accretion of sea-creature skeletons compressed over aeons. That information hit me in the heart in a good way. I thought back to my formative years in Indiana and the well water that I would drink by the gallon—water that had been steeped in the Hoosier limestone foundation. When I'd traveled back to South Bend, the first thing I would do was to drink glasses upon glasses of the well water—water from the earth, held by rock that was from the sea. I know now that water grounded me. Then I marveled that the very land on which I live in West Virginia is anchored into karst, a textured limestone.

Inside the abbey, the limestone hadn't just spoken to me . . . it had bellowed. Shouted me out of the grips of the previous lifetime that had hobbled me in this lifetime. How much more did I need or want to hear? I hesitated only a moment, then turned my back to the abbey wall so that I could experience the energy from the hills and hawthorn tree. I closed my eyes, then lifted my chin to take in the fragrance of the land, and feel on my face the ribbon of sun poking through the pouting clouds. I turned a palm to the stone, then leaned back for a full-body connection.

An orange haze like a tangerine chiffon scarf curtained the vision behind my eyes and suddenly, the face of my dead mother appeared. Though I'd had signs and nudges I felt she'd delivered, I'd never experienced an apparition before. My breath caught as I looked into her eyes and noticed her gentle smile. *Mom!* I bent forward and covered my still-closed eyes with my hands. Tears of joy and elation dampened my palms. In her travels, she was sure to have visited this popular landmark. Maybe the limestone had held the holograph of her, visible only to one on her wavelength. Maybe she'd come to comfort me after the psychic assault in the niche. *Mom! Mom! Mom!*

I reached back to the wall and lifted my head, eager to maintain connection to my mother in my motherland. But behind my eyes the orange had vanished. I felt empty in my gut and heart . . . hollow . . . and I knew that she was gone. Energetically and completely gone from me. "Ohhhh, Mom," I whispered urgently, "I needed more warning. Why didn't you give me any more warning you were leaving me?" My chest caved with silent sobbing. "I needed more warning."

My eyes streamed. My hands scrubbed at the wall, willing the stone to bring her back. "I'm still going to look for you, Mom," I whispered, head shaking away the abandonment, lower lip jutting out in childlike defiance. "I'm still. Going to. Look for you!"

I heard a voice in my head . . . not hers . . . but a compassionate voice: "You can look but there will be no more signs from her for you. It is time for you to come out from behind the shadow of your mother."

My shoulders slumped and my hands hung by my side. The voice continued: "You've hidden behind her. Hidden in her shadow. Hidden behind her large energy. And now it is time for you to stand on your own. She's no longer your excuse, and she's no longer on the pedestal. It's your time now."

*And just like that, I'm orphaned once again.*

The voice had one final message: "No, not orphaned. Now it is time to mother yourself."

∾

Back on the bus the others were sharing stories of their time at the abbey. It seemed as if everyone had some sort of dramatic reaction or experience. One woman said that as we were pulling up, she started to feel nauseous, and looked for a place to throw up. The woman who'd seemed frozen in place had in fact been unable to move for what she estimated was forty-five minutes. She too had a past-life experience so disturbing, she couldn't articulate the details.

I didn't want to share the details of my abbey experiences; I was still processing the finality of the loss of my mother in a way that I hadn't experienced when she left her human form. I had been grief-stricken then, wishing we'd gotten our relationship right before the final week of her life. But now, this full and complete departure hollowed me out.

As Fred expertly piloted us through the small towns and twisty roads of the Burren, I reflected about my birth people. I now understood they had no real meaning in my life; they were simply two-dimensional characters that advanced the plot of my experience of my mother. I realized that the real story was—and always had been—my relationship with my mother, Delphine, aka "The Duchess." Delphine, the queen mother shaping the daughter in preparation for her own sovereignty. I'd long been drawn to the Empress card in tarot; it felt like me—maternal, creative, abundant. Yet I had hesitated to claim it. Viewed through my ever-present lens of less-thanness, I was not worth keeping . . . not worth fighting for, as evidenced by the actions of my blood relatives. My very existence had been denied. I was meant to be hidden away forever in the dungeon of their shame. How could I even begin to see myself as the Empress . . . as a sovereign being of my own life?

Until the stone-cold moment of my mother's final departure, I'd felt I'd been missing a fundamental piece of myself that only the birth people could give me—that until I knew my lineage, I had no solid foundation on which to build self-sovereignty. Through all of the searching and striving and struggling trying to prove my value related to the birth people, I learned that I am like Dorothy from *The Wizard of Oz*—I had to go through the trials and tribulations to know that what I sought was not external . . . it was not about the birth people or absentee fathers . . . not even my bigger-than-life mother was responsible for my life and how I lived. It really was all up to me.

∽

Six months after my limestone revelations in Ireland, I was on the table of my massage therapist and energy healer, Tammy. I told her that in addition to attention to the perennial ache in my lower right back, I needed some energy work done around money issues—specifically what to charge for workshops that I would be doing at her transformational healing center. Tammy and I had a difference of opinion about what to charge; I wanted to offer the workshops at a third of the price she suggested. "You're going to need to bake something into me Reiki-wise so that I can energetically make your pricing work," I told her.

The bells on the sound machine chimed melodically, lulling me into a relaxed state. I felt Tammy scanning my energy, her hands like heat-seeking missiles. "I am getting there's an angel here, but I'm not familiar with her. I'll have to look her up to see what she helps with."

Eyes closed, I nodded, then asked, "What's her name?

"Delphine."

I laugh-cried so hard I could barely squeak out, "Delphine. Is. My. Mother." Tammy started laugh-crying too because though I'd shared the story of how my mother had left me in Ireland, I'd never referred to her by name. For fifteen minutes all we could do was laugh and cry. Finally I regained control. "Of *course* she would come back if it's something related to money . . . especially if I'm the one pushing for charging less!"

I felt euphoric the rest of the day—high-beam smile, snorts of bemused laughter, and hypersensitive sensory experiences. My mama was back! Back in my life in a different way, because I was different now. Stronger. Grounded. Sovereign. No doubt I could meet her as Empress to Duchess.

∾

Two months later, I went to an art retreat in southern Ohio. I'd gone in 2018 and had so thoroughly enjoyed the content and the location—a former retirement home for nuns—that I eagerly claimed a space for the August 2019 retreat. I hadn't been keen about the 2019 project—creating a doll that represented our personal muse—but Carolyn, the retreat leader, responded to my thoughtfully worded sentiment ("I don't want to make a fucking *doll*") with grace and good humor. Carolyn assured me that I could create whatever figure, symbol, or entity felt right to me.

I strolled across the Saint Mary's campus the first morning of the retreat, enjoying weather on the cusp between a Midwestern summer and fall—warm, dry, with a tinge of crispness. I ambled past the small limestone chapel and paused at the ornate wooden doors pondering whether to go in before visiting the labyrinth I'd heard was nearby. I decided against it and rounded the corner to a circular area ringed by a privet hedge. The labyrinth was a mere ten feet across—the smallest I'd experienced. I have an affinity for labyrinths, and I seek them out when I travel. I love the ritual of walking the circuitous path inward toward the center for release and back out with new awareness, knowledge, or peace of mind. A labyrinth is much different than a maze in that way; there is no way to get lost in a labyrinth—the path will always guide you in and out.

I stepped out of my Keen sandals and onto the perimeter of the gray pavers. My feet tensed and tingled from the grit, pine needles, and twigs sprinkled across the path. I paused at the opening, closed my eyes, and let Spirit know I was ready to release whatever needed releasing—to be in complete surrender. I opened my eyes and began mincing along, the tight turns precluding a normal stride.

Standing at the center, I looked toward the East, the rising sun beaming through the soft green leaves of some common shrub I probably should've known the name of. The light streaming through made it look like stained glass—chartreuse offset by emerald green where the leaves overlapped. I thought about how this part of Ohio felt very similar to the landscape of northern Indiana where'd I'd grown up.

No big aha came through, nor feeling of release of anything significant as I baby-stepped the tight concentric rings back to the beginning. *Maybe cuz the path was so short? I can't have walked for more than five minutes.* I brushed the bottom of one foot onto my denim-clad calf to dislodge the detritus, slid my clean foot into my sandal, then repeated the process with the other foot. I lost my balance, and as I wobbled my way upward, my body turned slightly. My gaze fell upon a statue the hedge had grown around and sheltered—Mary holding the baby Jesus.

My breath caught and I layered my hands over my heart. In that moment I understood it was my mother coming to me in the guise of the Holy Mother; Mom was, had been, and would always be my muse—an inspiration and an invitation to live fully . . . not in her way, but in mine. And I was her baby—pure, born without story . . . ready to make my own story . . . time to create my own story. Dizzy and giddy from the world-tilting, seismic, catalytic shift, I staggered to the chapel and bent to catch my breath. I blotted tears and snot with the hem of my cotton T-shirt, mentally applauding my mother . . . my Holy Mother . . . for her talent in manifesting mind-blowing mic-drop moments.

During the art retreat, I made, yes, a fucking *doll* . . . two, in fact: a Madonna dressed in shades of cornflower, periwinkle, and the ocean, and, enfolded in her arms, a baby swaddled in a fuchsia wrap embellished with words of power, freedom, and strength stamped in magenta. The baby wears a silver crown. Madonna and infant have a place of honor on my mantle. They are adorned and connected by a knotted blue-and-white rosary the retired nuns of Saint Mary's handcrafted from crochet thread.

Later at home, as I journaled about the art retreat experience, I reflected how Mary—the Blessed Virgin; Our Lady; the Holy Mother—had long been a thread connecting my mother and me. In my early years, it had been gossamer, spiderweb-thin—planting morning glories for her on Mother's Day; visiting the Fatima Shrine at Notre Dame; making a felt rosary pouch at age eight that she kept until her death. It was a rare artifact from my childhood; in fits of rage over the years, she'd thrown out most everything else I'd made or bought her.

After our reconciliation in my forties, Mom gave me a beautiful crystal rosary she'd picked up during her travels to the Czech Republic and, later, one made from roses she'd purchased on a visit to Medjugorje, a famous pilgrimage destination for devotees of Mary.

I marveled that my birth mother's name is Mary, and that through the Blessed Virgin Mary, I am connected to my mother, Delphine. We were all stitched together through motherhood, divine or biological. I can see now how my birth mother played a small, insignificant part in the merry band of Marys; my mother had the starring role. Through this Holy Mother experience, I recognized I could finally drop all the victim stuff, all the enmity, all the hurt. I am that pure baby, wrapped in power, strength, and freedom. I can grow into anyone and anything.

I started to close the journal, then remembered something else. As I was regaining my equilibrium in front of the chapel after the Holy Mother incident, I'd noticed a dark form at my feet—a cicada about two inches long with green tribal markings and fragile iridescent wings. Though the familiar buzzy song of cicadas was in full swing, it had been a surprise to see one parked on the threshold of the chapel. I wondered what symbolism was associated with that insect. It surprised me that after nearly a decade of living on Cicada Drive, I'd never before looked up the metaphysical meaning of the noisy bugs.

After seeing the results of the Google search about cicadas, I sobbed with laughter, thinking once again of my mother's dramatic showmanship from beyond. Nearly ten years earlier, the Cicada Drive house popped up at the top of a list of houses for sale, though it met none of the search parameters I'd entered. It was well above my price point, twice as many acres as my rural loan was approved for, and had no bathroom on the main level . . . yet there it was. I knew it was my house the minute it displayed on the screen, even though a sale was pending. I argued with my realtor, who resisted calling the listing agent—"I've got to see it. I know it's mine."

She convinced the listing agent to show me the property. When I walked in, I knew I was home. Soaring cathedral ceilings clad in cedar. Well-loved pine floors. Tall windows and French doors providing a nearly uninterrupted view of the heavily forested holler, including an ancient and massive oak tree. As I gazed up and around, drinking in the natural splendor of the place, a breeze wafted through the open windows, carrying the unmistakable scent of my mother—a blend of Youth Dew, Virginia Slims, and syrupy wine. Later that afternoon, the pending contract fell through and I made a successful bid using the money finally released from my mother's estate after two years of waiting. The amount was a big-enough down payment to bring the mortgage down to a dollar figure I could handle on my limited income.

Without Mom, I could never have afforded the Cicada Drive house. My home has been a sanctuary and my stability these past years . . . a solid foundation to support me as I've searched and grown and healed and transformed. I spent months as a hermit in my home, slowly gathering the strength and knowledge to emerge new and whole.

What I learned about the metaphysical meaning of cicadas is that they are a symbol of rebirth. They undergo a long period of gestation underground before they emerge to sing their distinctive song. To sing the song that only they can sing.

And so . . . I sing.

# Couldn't Have Done It Without You (aka Acknowledgments) Page

Though silly, one of the first things I turn to in any book is the Acknowledgments page, hoping to see my name. Silly because there'd be no earthly reason for my name to be there. . . and yet.

So, if you do the same thing—Here is your name! I acknowledge you right here in print (or pixels or voice, depending on how you're consuming this.)

Deepest gratitude to Christina Baldwin for the container you created during the Self as the Source of Story retreat that allowed me to craft a critical chapter I'd been reluctant to write. Profound thanks for the insightful question you asked that changed the trajectory of the story.

So much gratitude to Linda Joy Meyers who rode in the front car of my writing roller coaster. I am thankful you kept climbing aboard despite my ups and downs. Your input and editorial eye on my many drafts were invaluable.

Hugs and gratitude to the facilitators and participants of the writing groups and retreats who tenderly nurtured or helped prune early drafts. . . or endured my whining about my early drafts.

A deep bow of appreciation for Brooke Warner and the opportunity to publish through She Writes Press. Appreciation too for the generous support of the She Writes Press community, particularly the Fall 2022 cohort, and specifically, my memoir-writing sisters, Annie Chappell, Amy Turner, Isidra Mencos, Joanne Kelly, and Linda Broder. Pause here and go buy all the She Writes Press books!

Ten toes up to Dene Neal who quite literally sat at my feet and cheered me on to keep writing.

Tammy Godette, she of the holy healing hands, deepest gratitude for the myriad mystical ways you guided and supported me as I navigated all the realms.

Rebecca Word—gurrrrrl, I'da been roadkill ten times over without your wisdom and potions. Thanks for helping me cross the finish line in fine fettle.

To my ever-welcoming South Bend Byrne people, especially Terry and Bunny—I am so grateful for your unfailing love and acceptance, no matter the time, place, or circumstances.

To my first readers, Beth Wilson, Caity Byrne, Kelly Byrne, Linda Zupan, Marla Schlaffer, and Tracy Labrie—buckets of blessings and thanks for your thoughtful and extremely helpful feedback. Your respective perspectives were instrumental in refining and clarifying my story.

To those who've patiently held space, listened long, offered a shoulder, taken my side, and gamely looked through the microscope each time I dissected another part of my story—there just aren't thanks enough: Caity, Carolyn Carter, Carolyn Crofoot (wish you were still on the earthly plane to receive this sentiment,) Chrissy Currier, Courtney West, Dawn Downey, Kelly, Linda, Marla, Squeaky, Sukhwant Shimkaveg, Suzanne Wise, and Tracy.

Hugs and hearts to my Surrender Circle sisters, Carolyn and Linda, for weekly doses of love, witnessing, and prayers. Special thanks to my Heart Sister for all the extra helpings.

Wonder Woman—or Tracy, as you're known to mere mortals— you are a marathoner, both as a runner and as a friend. Eternal gratitude for going the distance, especially when it was difficult and painful. And soul-deep thanks for introducing me to my two favorite coasts—NorCal and Ireland.

To my bestie, Beth, XOXOXOXO and oodles of love for all of the above, and for hours of porching, beaching, arting, card consulting, digging deep, burning baboon butts, and finding our next favorite place.

To my one and only sister…my first baby. Good morning! Endless appreciation for hours-long 5-minute calls; Zoomba sessions; dental advice; gifties and confetti; wiener dog memes; and 50 ways to use shotgun-blasted 55-gallon drums. You…you are a ding-dong…and, I couldn't love you more.

To my son, Kelly, you often bring tears to my eyes through your humility about your heroics, and devotion to the girls and women in your life. And other times…because of your pull-no-punches-jackhammer-of-logic pronouncements. So much love and clouds of unicorn farts to you my Sweet Boy. And to Girl Kelly, love and admiration for your quiet strength, being a role model mother, and allowing whatever happens at grandma's to stay at grandma's.

To my daughter, Caity, Platinum status for both the practical—first reader, first editor, boss—and the personal—brilliant, hilarious, fashion-forward, crazy cat mom, buttectomy-britches-wearing ride or die. You may once have been a Mini-Me but you is all you now. I like you so very very much. Mwah, mwah, mwah. And to Matt, who thank the Goddess, has taken over tending to your welfare, and who is the best son-in-law and wasp eradicator a Mumsie could wish for.

To my grandchildren—including grandsouls—who embiggen my heart. Corrina and Jillian, you are THE most amazing, interesting, thoughtful, generous, creative, fun, and loving young women. You are my constant joy. Love you! Love you! Love you!

And finally, thanks, Mom. . . I really couldn't have done it without you.

# The Red Thread

The red thread (sometimes referred to as the red cord, or red string) has multiple meanings across different cultures and belief systems.

Basically, though, the common thread—so to speak—is connection.

Connection to a person, soul mate, Source energy, luck, desires, or protector.

For me, the red thread on the cover of the book reflects the legend that says:

An invisible red thread connects those destined to meet, regardless of time, place, or circumstance. The thread may stretch or tangle, but will never break.

If you are reading this, we were destined to meet if only through my story!

In acknowledgement of my gratitude that we are connected (and that you read this far!) it is my honor to offer you a wee giftie.

Send an email to: regiftedmemoir@gmail.com with your name and postal mailing address and I will send you a little prezzie I make with my own two hands.

No charge. No shenanigans with your personal information. No strings attached. (Sorry...couldn't resist the pun!)

Hand to heart,

Candi

# About the Author

photo credit: Mary Kate McKenna, The Uncorporate Headshot

Candi Byrne is a gregarious introvert, nomadic homebody, and pragmatic woowooist. She lives in an enchanted forest on the south side of North Mountain in the Eastern Panhandle of West Virginia. Her cozy, colorful cottage contains a bounty of art supplies for the "Magic on the Mountain" creative retreats she facilitates, as well as the "Let's Get Messy" sleepovers she has regularly with her two granddaughters, who live over the creek and through the woods.

# SELECTED TITLES FROM SHE WRITES PRESS

She Writes Press is an independent publishing company founded to serve women writers everywhere. Visit us at www.shewritespress.com.

*Twice a Daughter: A Search for Identity, Family, and Belonging* by Julie McGue. $16.95, 978-1-64742-050-5

When adopted twin Julie faces several serious health issues at age forty-eight, she sets out to find her birth parents and finally gets the family medical history she's lacking—and she ends up on a years-long quest that ultimately reveals much more than she bargained for.

*All the Sweeter: Families Share Their Stories of Adopting from Foster Care* by Jean Minton. $16.95, 978-1-63152-495-0

The stories of twelve families who have adopted one or more children from the US foster care system, accompanied by topical chapters that explore the common challenges these families face, including the complications that accompany transracial adoptions, helping children understand adoption, relationships with birth parents, and raising a traumatized child.

*Emma's Laugh: The Gift of Second Chances* by Diana Kupershmit $16.95, 978-1-64742-112-0

After Diana's first child, Emma, is born with a rare genetic disorder, Diana relinquishes her to an adoptive family, convinced they will parent and love Emma better than she ever could—but when fate intervenes and the adoption is reversed, bringing Emma back home, Diana experiences the healing and redemptive power of love.

*Fixing the Fates: An Adoptee's Story of Truth and Lies* by Diane Dewey. Since being surrendered in a German orphanage forty-seven years ago, Diane Dewey has lived with her adoptive parents near Philadelphia—loved, but deprived of information about her roots. When her Swiss biological father locates her, their reunion becomes an obsession—and ultimately leads her to the answers, and peace, she's been seeking.